The Wanderer's Guide to Consciousness

Consciousness

A Spirit's Memo.

♥

E. Marie Kelly

Dedicated...

To my teacher who's my student,
The stranger who's my friend,
The person in the mirror,
The one standing in the end.
To the blank page in my book,
The chapter that came before,
To the one who kept me caged,
The one who helped me soar.
 To the seat that was reserved,
The person who kept my place.
The one who made me run,
And the person who finished the race.
To those footprints I couldn't fill and the ones I
couldn't wash away,
To everyone I may have missed,
May you all be blessed in life in every single way!

Contents

You are standing on the shore; the sweet smell of the oceans musk is misting your nose. The beautiful sound of birds hovers above your head. You are waiting in line with your family and friends to board a boat to take you to where you have wanted to go for a long time. Finally you get up to the front and your family is parting ways as well as your friends, each choosing a different boat to board. You have a choice to make; two boats sit in front of you. One a humble small boat with a motor that can go fast but very little of your belongings can be taken aboard; the second a giant cruise ship, enough room for you and all your belongings, without feeling cramped. Very few people pass up the cruise ship, pulling aboard their large suitcases and lavish possessions. Most of your friends and family members board the cruise ship. You ponder which boat to board. Both ensure a safe trip to your final destination, the larger one a little bit more comfortable than the small one; however the smaller one ensures that you will reach your destination quicker. This is the journey you have been waiting for all your life, yet it is where your life will begin, you desire to reach your destination as quickly as possible, but you are fearful of letting go of your possessions and not being surrounded in luxury and your companions. You envision taking the cruise ship and you imagine extravagant parties, lots of funand never being far from entertainment. You then foresee as time passes more and more people get more and more agitated with each other. Days turn into months, months into years and this boat no longer houses the paradise you boarded. Then you envision life on the smaller boat, you have to ration all of your food, your belongings left behindand while it is very uncomfortable the people aboard are humble and graceful, you all get a long, through sharing in a rough lonely life. You grow close to these people on the shorter trip. You reach your destination quicker and are so much more appreciative of the beauty of the journey and of what has awaited you. Then you wake up.

Upon awakening from the dream of "reality" your life comes to grips with a lot of concepts and emotions. Upon awakening I realized how flawed the perception of "consciousness" is. You see all around you people whom are open and conscious and happy and you wonder secretly to yourself how on earth they are happy while all the problems in the physical world still persist. The rent is still due, the kids are still there, the unhappy marriage is still intact. You go through a painful journey of discovery in which you discover; how bad a parent you were-how you messed up so much with your kids, how you locked yourself to this person *forever* without even knowing who you yourself was to begin with, you see the house that is a drain on your energy, the monotonous job, you know you must face your karma to undo the distress in your life, but all you can do is mourn, grieve and wonder, "where do I start?"

The journey to conscious living is trying, hard and sometimes physically unbearable, yet so possible! YOU are the one YOU have been waiting for, that void, that answer you've been searching for, it has always been right under your nose...literally! You see these words and start to feel a flicker in your heart, me? Really me? I'm not good enough, I am a horrible person, but yet, you are the savior you have been waiting for!

To prepare for this life changing event it is like a warrior preparing for battle, for this is the journey that awaits you; a physical, mental, emotional and spiritual battle. For so many and for so long we have allowed others to be victorious in our battles, will you let them win the war for you?

Part I

Waking up

The first stage in consciousness is waking up. You have been caught in a dream for so long, where everything you perceive, everything you feel, has all been glazed over by dream state. Imagine when you first wake up in the morning, your alarm goes off. The first thing you hear in the morning is that siren blasting in your head, you open your eyes, roll over look at the time, perhaps you hit the snooze a couple of times, hearing the siren over and over until you look at the clock realized you've overslept and it's time to get up RIGHT NOW! However groggy or disturbed you feel you know you have no time to react because there is so little left. We find that in consciousness both journeys are very similar to these reactions, some people get up as soon as the alarm goes off, some people hit the snooze over and over until they realize "oh no the time is now." Whichever way you came to be awake neither way is wrong as long as you learned something along the way.

The awakening process is much like the grieving process your life barrels through different areas, sometimes bouncing in between two or more emotional states, sometimes quick, sometimes very long. It is all dependent on how you take things and how you have handled things in the past. Grieving is normal, after all, everything you have known in your life is dying, mourn over it and celebrate the rebirth of YOU!

In the grieving process there are 7 steps to regain your life, they are as follows:
   1.   Shock and Denial
   2.   Pain and Guilt
   3.   Anger and Bargaining

4. Depression, Reflection, Loneliness
5. The Upward Turn
6. Reconstruction and Working Through
7. Acceptance and Hope

While each is according to you, these are the general areas in which you will feel your emotions pulling.

Shock and Denial

Waking up for me didn't happen in one foul swoop, it was years in the making and happened over a series of events, I didn't have one AHA moment that said, yes this is how it works, although through my journey there have been AHA moments that gave me strength and the determination to see this through. My first experiences all cultivated fear. I saw the world how it was, I saw evil in its true depth (and now I recognize the beauty of evil)and I felt very scared that it was too late for me to rectify the situation that I had created.

I grew up attending a Catholic school, raised in a very Irish Catholic family and had all these illusions of what it meant to be a good person. A good person attended mass, they gave away their money, they confessed their sins to the man behind the curtain, they knew all the prayers and took on the problems of others as "their cross to bear in the world."

In my teenage years I began experimenting with drugs and while the highs were the most amazing thing I had felt thus far, a part of me hated myself because I was in need of the high to be happy. Throughout the years I began losing people, very quickly, almost seemed as it was all together. I resorted to more drugs and a true anger at the God I had been raised to always love. I felt this spite and anger towards every living being, every reflection of God, I said "fuck this all, if God was real he wouldn't wish this pain on me, I wouldn't lose anyone and I would be happy without drugs. I'd always be high." Looking back I can see how this was my lowest point, but my ego was at its strongest. I did what I wanted to do, because I felt there were no repercussions in the end for any of my actions. Fuck the world was my motto and I lived it in every breath. I didn't help others; I helped myself, only me at any cost to someone else. I pushed everyone in my life that I loved away so that I could never be hurt by anyone.

The first instance where something behind the veil revealed itself to me I was terrified and in shock. I had been grounded, everything in my room had been removed and I was threatened with criminal charges. The first night coming off drugs and being faced with *reality* I cried laying in my bed, I begged God, whoever he was, to take my life, to end it because I didn't have the strength to, nor to carry on. I begged and cried for what must have been a short time; however it felt like the longest scope of time. In an instant I felt this collision through my body, dread and even more pain filled me. I was all of a sudden surrounded by hundreds of queen ants flying all around me and I heard this sinister laugh, this laugh that to this day I could hear and have an AHA moment. At the time it was the most terrifying thing I had ever heard. I began praying, "Just kidding, just kidding," I repeated, "I don't want to die, Grandma, Janine, if you're hearing me, help me, tell God I don't want to die." In that instance the swarm around me dropped dead, I felt a calming peace and I could smell my Grandma. I jumped out of bed, not believing what I was looking at, feeling, that high, that peace. I went and grabbed my little brother to verify I was not hallucinating and in fact was staring at a million of dead ants. He agreed that they were there and then I had him vacuum them all up because I just couldn't believe the entire picture. Though I had changed my addictions I had really put that incident out of my mind, I hit snooze on the alarm and ignored that anything outside of the ants had ever really happened.

Some time went by I acknowledged that there was something, but I really denied that I could ever grasp what it was. I could never fathom how deep the rabbit hole went so why try is how I came to terms with it. The next event culminated with a boy, "Zombie." This boy somehow was able to say everything that I had always kind of felt, his vast awareness and knowledge of the universe astounded me and it pushed me to great lengths to pursue him, but truly what I wanted was that knowledge. I wanted to hear everything he thought, because if he was able to say all these things then what else was he hiding in his thoughts?

We dated for a short time in which my fascination with the paranormal grew. He was so unafraid and ready to face whatever right in the eye, he believed in aliens and had talked about how he'd seen quite a few, he talked about spirituality, evil and good. He knew science inside and out, he was great with math and he was so intriguing and pushed me to great heights to begin again to question my reality. It is time again I thought, I believe it's out there and now have the confidence to pursue it. That confidence quickly shrank back down when I found that just because I opened myself up to it didn't mean it would suddenly be revealed, I wouldn't see aliens or have discussions with Nikola Tesla and suddenly understand the universe. Again I was back in bed hitting the snooze, "if we are all so special how come some got things I didn't? I didn't want a negative force to slam through my body, would much rather have the glamorized versions of spirituality!"

As time went on I turned into a recluse. I really saw everyone I knew as ignorant and so self-consumed to really see what was going on in the world. I hated others for their disregard and for their lack of realization; people had instances all the time hitting themselves in the face and yet didn't care or denied that part of them. I was the ultimate conspiracy theorist and knew every little plot the Illuminati was using to destroy humanity or rule it. I saw 2012 and was sure it was going to be a catastrophe! All the signs pointed to it so it must have been true. This phase lasted approximately two years of my life.

Pain and Guilt

A pen pal of mine sent me a video that would change my life forever, a conspiracy theorist himself he said he found a video that I would enjoy and had to watch. It was called the <u>2012 Enigma</u>. It was a one hour video on YouTube divided into sections of ten minutes of some dude (David Wilcock) just talking. I hadn't really been into lectures ever but within the first ten minutes I was so hooked I kept clicking on the next video in the series, the next, the next and so on. David spoke of the grand things that Zombie had always spoke of, but to such a depth and with such an understanding he mesmerized me so much more than Zombie had. He not only dropped this huge load on my lap, but he also explained everything he spoke of in such a way that it was so easy to grasp. I felt like a genius because all of a sudden I could speak of DNA and molecules and all these very complex ideas with an understanding behind them. He also spoke of something else, of how fear is used to control us and others. He spoke of the Egyptians and the beauty of 2012 and all of a sudden my view was changed from fear to love. I welcomed 2012. While this realization was a great moment in my life, it didn't change what I had been doing. I had been spreading fear to others.

I began looking in depth at every little instance that I used to control someone else, every little time that I had gone against the free will principle, which according to David Wilcock is, "The greatest gift that this being (God) has given us is the opportunity to discover we are one with it in our own way, without anyone telling us what to believe or what to do or how to think, it's our path and we can do anything we want, if we start infringing on someone else's free will, it is a design of the universe that whatever we measure out to others will come back to ourselves. You can practice the negative path if you want to. You can infringe on someone else's freewill you can manipulate them, you can lie to them, you can steal from them, leave them unemployed and homeless and hungry, but you will be stolen from, lied too, manipulated, controlled…" I felt a deep remorse for what I had done. I thought how on earth could I ever take back all the poison I had spread? How could I now stand on my same soap box and tell others that "hey just kidding this is the truth, you are beautiful and have nothing to fear?" How could I take back the times that I had infringed on someone's free will?

Anger and Bargaining

I went straight into anger and bargaining, I once again hated myself, even though I knew I was beautiful and perfect and endless possibilities were in front of me I couldn't see past my anger to allow myself to pursue what I was sent to do. I bargained time and time again, "if you donate money here it will help you take back what you did. If you tell these people this, then it will help you rectify the situation. If you swear off this it will help you be better…"

Depression, Reflection and Loneliness

I went through a period of depression; I was depressed I could betray people I loved so deeply. I kept myself secluded from those that I had wronged because I felt so unworthy of forgiveness, of compassion, of joy. An ex-boyfriend and fair weather friend from years before came to my house one day, he hadn't known how to get a hold of me so he just showed up, "Prophet". He had been a friend with whom I had partied with in the days of old and all of a sudden he had found this great joy in his life. He had found God. I thought, how preposterous, you can't find him, he is always there and more so I really didn't believe in the "religious" God. I obliged him though, I thought at least don't affect his free will to believe what he wanted. I went to a couple of Non-Denominational services with him, all the while secretly scoffing at the idea of dancing hand in hand around the room and listening to a bunch of people tell you why you were going to hell and trying to cast out your demons. It was as if I was watching a movie of all this supposed happiness when really they were all feeding off condemning others, hypocrisy. As much as I disagreed with the views of the people at his church it felt good to be around people who celebrated-their version- of spirituality!

It happened on Mother's Day, I came home about 1 am just after hanging out with Prophet, he told me just before I went inside, "remember, Jesus is the son of God." And I jokingly replied, "Remember, I don't know what to believe." When I got in I thought about how if this was all real how I would like to have that moment so much to just be like, "yes I'm saved, thank the Lord!" I got into bed and felt something jabbing me, I pulled out a little angel figurine and laughed as I set it on my nightstand. I laid down and truly prayed, I said, "If you're out there I want to know, if you're so great show me." I went to bed and while I dreamt that night I dreamt I was sitting on an altar with Jesus, He was talking to me, said some things I have shared with very few and pointed at me and said "I have to let you go now." Just then I woke up and the bed was slamming against the ground and wall, shaking violently, I tried to move but the harder I tried the more I felt resisted. I heard that laugh, that sinister laugh so many years back I had heard, I heard "you'll never escape," throughout the laughter and the slamming. I told myself over and over, "this is a dream, wake up, you're dreaming, just wake up. I began to scream, "Help me! HELP ME!" No one came. I then began to pray, "Jesus save me." I don't know how long I was praying because the evil tension seemed to slip away, there was this light I focused on, that got brighter and brighter and began coming closer to me. I felt this warmth and in an instant had forgotten what had just happened to me, the light grew and eventually I was sitting in the presence of divine peace and love. I didn't try to process it at all; I just soaked up this beautiful feeling this loving feeling. As that feeling passed I grabbed my dream journal I began to scribble ferociously everything that had just happened not trying to filter or understand any of it, just allowing the experience to flow freely from pen to paper. I sat up for a short time in the wee hours of the morning (my timeline for this from awake to sleep again approximately 2 am- 4 am).

The next day I had little time to think of what had happened, I had to get up and make a ham roast for mom and was already well behind schedule, I put it out of my mind until later in the evening when the events for the day were over. I sat on my bed, read my dream journal, sure it was all a dream and I thought if it was real I would have written it in my journal and then I saw everything written down, not remembering I had written it at all. I then tried to explain it off, I was having a seizure, so I laid down and shook, didn't make the same movement or sound, I sat up and hopped up and down, no dice, the only thing that made the sound was when I stood at the bottom and held the posts and slammed it back and forth.

When I told Prophet of what had happened he rejoiced, he told me that night he stayed up for 4 hours praying for me and my soul. I thought wow, I am so lucky to have had the Hand of God come down and touch me in such a way that singles me out for some greatness. A short couple of months went by and I did the Christian thing, I attended church (a couple of different kinds because I didn't know which one fit for me) and I read scripture all the while suppressing the beliefs I had before, that I was perfect, that I was a reflection of God, even though these things are in The Bible the Christian ideal is to teach you that you are full of sin and not even close to what God resembles. I don't argue that we can never comprehend the AWEsome of our Divine Creator, but I believe that we were created in His image and that we are and always will be a part of him. Prophet and I had a falling out and I was left alone, I no longer had the one person that I shared the connection of God with and I said, "well God, now my only friend has left me, you know how I hate to be alone, so if you want me to continue to do your work put people in my life that are going to help me on your path."

The Upward Turn

Oh man, were my prayers answered...well sort of...I wanted Christian people, instead what I got was "pagans," Buddhists popped up in my life, Taoist, Agnostics, non-secular conscious people, Atheists, people with varying beliefs all living their own spiritual journey, just in different ways. It culminated for me when I learned of my coworker planning to open a non-profit in Africa. I had longed to open up a spiritual center in Colorado in hopes that people could come, be themselves, believe what they wanted, share love and not money. I began to see myself in others and love them more and more for their differences, for their similarities, I saw myself in each of them and I returned to being optimistic about my future.

Again, I met a boy "Mr. Happy", he was so open and so full of love that I quickly grew to love him. I mean in a matter of days I had this burning sensation whenever I thought or talked to him. He had so many beliefs that left an impression on me so much. He was working on reconstructing his life and he had such gifts that I could not put down on paper. He was cutting his physical addictions and loving life even when life was not so kind to him. He embraced who I was and truly helped me overcome the self-doubt I had always struggled with. He taught me how beautiful I was and we explored the world together as children, new to everything our eyes touched.

Within a few months we moved in together, while before we had spats that were quickly resolved nothing could have prepared me for how life would turn out after moving in together. The first day was hell, I felt my solar plexus close up tight while he was at work and I was confronted by his Grandma and his brother on two separate issues at the same time. I tried my best to remain neutral while Mr. Happy was at work. I wanted him to be there for the decision making, he had put so much into this new place and I saw his glory being threatened. It seemed to work out and when he came home I was relieved that he was there and would be able to handle the situation. Within the first couple of days I was faced with another instance where it closed up, a friend of his was helping us move and had asked me "how do you like finally having your own place," (I had always lived with my family before this), I said, "well, I don't know yet, I've always had a lot of people and I like it, but I'm going to have to get used to it." I didn't know why this gave him such a reaction but Mr. Happy attacked me, "well you can always move back, your name isn't on the lease." I felt hurt, here was this guy that was supposed to be sympathetic and understanding for how I was feeling, I mean it was a separate grieving time for me because I felt as though the child within was finally dead, now it was time to be a grown up, take on grown up responsibilities and all he could do is tell me, "you failed at being a grown up, go back."

It was little instances that I began to distrust myself again and more so Mr. Happy, I thought I knew you so very little and now I am stuck here, new place far from my friends and family and I'm stuck with you, who doesn't know or love me at all. More blows began to come when I would be at home cleaning, arranging things, just so when he would come home everything would be perfect and he could relax. So I could spend some time with him, the time I had desperately been craving since he had been working and our schedules were clashing. I felt exhausted I thought "I've created this perfect place for you to come and all you ever want to do is go to the bar." Happy, His brother and his brother's girlfriend were the only people aside from phone calls I had daily interaction with, I felt trapped and to add insult to injury I was once told by someone, "if you were a better girlfriend you could get him to quit going out every night and drinking." I was so crushed by those words because I thought, HOW? How can I be better, I clean, I make breakfast, dinner, I don't tell him "NO YOU CAN'T." (Going back to the free will principle.) What more can I do? I began feeling resentment, here is your paradise and you shit all over it, here is me offering you everything I can give and you don't want any of it. Moreover I never shared the deep pain I was in, I never told him how hurt I was, until one night.

All the negative energy I was holding in culminated and led up to me breaking when he made a comment about me getting liposuction. I didn't know what to do I just responded, "that's all you've said to me lately is everything about my weight." It was already a sore wound considering everyone in my life had always ridiculed my weight whether I'm too skinny or too fat; it had always been a deep struggle. It seemed that entire week every conversation we shared he would say something about my weight.

I went inside and just cried, he tried to fix things, but it was too late, I had gone back to how I felt before him, I hated everything about me, now more so, because the one person I had finally felt I could be myself around hated me too. That's why, I thought, why he's never here; he can't stand the sight of me. I left that night only to drown my sorrows in booze.

We worked things out, but we just hit the tip of the iceberg. Then Christmas came. While trying to figure out plans for it I felt a little hurt, because I had always spent Christmas with MY family and now trying to share it with another family (whom yes I did love) was so frustrating. It ended up us splitting and he went to his, I went to mine. I got drunk and by the time he came to pick me up I was well past ready to listen to him, the person who tricked me into living with him only to reveal he thinks I'm ugly and fat and the list went on and on. I bitched him out for who knows how long, he left and I called my best friend. She told me to calm down, wait for the morning she would get me and I could cool down. After an hour I saw him drive by, I got off the phone with her and called my mom to come pick me up. I wrote an angry letter, I packed my things and an hour after was on my way out. Perhaps he could feel me, he texted right after and asked if I had my id, I told him to have fun drinking. I was so sure I hated him.

How could he leave me on Christmas? Who cares if I was drunk, he picked me up from having a good time with my family to just leave me alone once again, on Christmas. There was no reasoning with my logic, I felt completely vindicated.

The next day was a rude awakening. I made a complete circle and was back to square one. I was so convinced he was wrong and I was right and torn because I loved him, or believed it was love. We projected our reality on one another and truly, I don't feel either one of us was loving one another. To the definition of love. I love him more today than I ever did in our relationship, it is because now I see the beauty more clearly in all beings, yes, sometimes the picture still gets blurred, but because I honor my own beauty so much more I am able to honor the beauty in all creatures so much easier! We tried for another month or so after to talk and make things work, we were more honest with each other (and possibly ourselves) than what we had been for at least a couple of months and then it ended. Kind of, ex-lover and some kind of friend he will remain, I am learning to love myself now.

Reconstruction and Working Through

I look back at the perfection that was attained in my relationship with Mr. Happy in the beginning, I know where I failed, I can point and say he did this, but truly if I don't let go and forgive Mr. Happy I may always deny myself the love and respect I deserve. I gave Mr. Happy what I thought was a perfect world. What I thought was happiness. It wasn't for him and more so I wasn't meant to give it to him in the first place, because I drained my energy on it and I placed a million expectations on Mr. Happy. I believe where I have the chance to really work on for the future is not placing people and actions into categories, wrong or right. Being so stuck on how others are wrong and right took the power away from me. I gave them the power to do wrong against me, it is now time to retake my power and regain each piece of me I have given away, to restore myself back to the whole person I want to be. I smile on the fond memories and while yes, painful ones exist too, they are no longer my captive, because I love ME and how I show MYSELF that I love ME is by letting go of the pain, forgiving everyone involved and moving forward with what the world has to offer.

I think it is highly important for your sanity to face the reality of pain. You have created this painful world you live in and the universe is very generous, in that He gives you exactly what you need. This pain in my life was given to me because I had asked for it, I had longed for all this pain to be mine. To have the big melodrama of life played out like an awesome screen play. I got it all.

Acceptance and Hope

While acceptance is part of the answer, I believe that hope is just as friendly as fear. If you think of it, you accept what happened, then what, "I'm just going to hope for the best." Really? How do you hope? You close your eyes and think; okay hopefully this is what happens. What hope does is prepare us for the best scenario. When, face it, the best scenario is not always possible, at least when you're sitting around hoping for it. Hope alone is not enough to suffice for living, if you have hope alone you will believe that you never have to work to get what you want.

Think of every person who's ever inspired you, were they just hoping someone would give them the answer? Were they hoping for a better world? We can hope all we want, but life will not change or get better if you don't get involved in action. Hope is an excuse for us to sit around and do nothing.

My action now, is to accept and move forward, my action is to go into the world guns blazing (and yes the metaphoric ones) and change it, I'm not going to hope that Ghandi or Jesus are going to come back and save this shitty world we live in, because it might not happen, or it may happen, but maybe not in my lifetime. What am I doing? Writing, painting, singing, loving, I am rekindling that relationship I lost with myself by rediscovering what helps keep me balanced. I have given my surroundings a face lift, cut out the excess items I don't need to make way for the things I do need. I love to paint and yet I do it so little, so what did I do the other day? I cleared my schedule to paint, to learn to love to be around me so I will have more energy to love to be around others. I am rekindling my love for myself it is my only goal right now, for I understand that I don't have the energy right now for anything else.

What next?

As many will agree you just don't reach enlightenment and your growth stops. I used to view it as this, as if one day it will just open for me and everything would be clear, the more I open the more I find that this was a big misconception on my part. Each day it seems as though the struggles get a little more confusing on how to solve and a little more of a weight on my heart. I rise with the understanding and the knowledge of how to handle situations and how I can grow from each moment, but I am constantly perplexed when I face those instances in particularly vulnerable moments.

Part of consciousness is the subconscious sending a message to the world saying "I am ready for more." When the world gives me more I often have the reaction of, "Why now? Everything was just looking so up?" It's taken me shorter intervals to recover from moments of pain as it had in the past and I find myself facing them more honestly than I had in the past. I check in with my heart, because regardless of how open I become with myself and the world my heart still feels the pain, possibly now more than ever because I have begun to become more aware of how connected I am with every living being and our Creator.

Part II

Architecture

Everyone tells you these fantastic stories of how they found themselves and how they have become so awake and aware as if it had happened overnight. Nothing so big happens overnight. It will take diligence, dedication and planning, for you to become the change you want to see. What is the first step? Well planning of course. You have to plan in order to make any change. Whether it is in your head or on paper you have to come up with a plan. Become the architecture of your life!

You must evaluate your entire life, be truthful with yourself, brutally honest! Evaluate your relationships, your likes and dislikes, what you NEED in life to be happy and healthy, what you WANT in life to be healthy and happy, why you haven't done these things, if you haven't, or why these things are such an intricate part of your life.

I believe that you're DNA and your main seven chakras are closely tied together. Imagine each chakra as a circle and they are lined up, now uncoil the Crown Chakra and the Root Chakra and place each on either side of the remaining chakras, the picture that appears is a DNA strand. You have your physical being and your spiritual being and within the line you have your mental body and emotional body. Imagine the spiritual line is broken; your DNA will look misshaped and sick. If you remove a bar, like a piece of your mental state the same problem presents. This is why your health in all areas of your life is important to balance and keep. They all live in harmony and if part of you is sick or unhealthy it affects all areas of your life. Imagine that your physical, mental, emotional and spiritual are all separate beings apart of you. Each one is in need of attention and dedication and each one can only be satisfied by you.

When you begin to architect your life these are the areas of focus that you should begin with. I have had a hard time transitioning my life from being driven and focused on others, but have realized I have four beings I already have to care for and if I don't show them attention they will certainly not cooperate fully in showing attention to others. You cannot heal the world if you have no energy to heal yourself. You must start with your own self, if you say well helping others helps me, that is fine and you need to find what things make you perform at your best in life, but if when you continually reach out to help others you find that your draining your own energy reserves then you are not truly helping them. It requires no extra energy to truly help people then what you have.

Envision it this way, if you work with someone that always comes to you to get their job done and you are continually putting off your own projects and deadlines to be a "team player" and help them, eventually your own work starts to stack up and you may get fired because of it while they are living unchallenged and looking good in the boss' eyes. With your personal life it is the same. If you are continuously putting your needs on the back burner so that someone else can be satisfied your needs pile up. Then when you finally get a chance to sort through them it feels unmanageable, you say "I cannot do all of this in my life time." When if you were meeting all of your "deadlines" to begin with there would not be a major stack and you would even find yourself with extra time to devote to others. This whole concept is very conflicting, do I help or do I worry solely about myself?

Start with you to make the decision. If your coworker asks you to get a project done and you say, "I'm sorry I have my own work to do," it is not selfish. You need to get your work done and take care of you; your coworker is responsible for their work and needs to take care of them. If you have the ability to support them, offer insight for the easiest way to accomplish something or take one piece of their project into your responsibility, it is still up to you to accept, if it is only going to stress your workload, decline. No one will resent you for declining, because ultimately it is their burden to bear. If you complete your tasks at your work the whole work place benefits from it, just as if you complete your needs in life the whole world benefits. A very close friend of mine was in a financial pickle years ago around the winter holidays. She didn't openly ask for my help, but with the way I had always been in my life and I had naturally said, "I can rearrange my budget, help you with rent and figure it out." Close to two years had gone by before she ever paid me back, I didn't know how to ask her for the money, I wanted to keep our relationship intact, but there were many occasions I needed that money. Honestly, I should have never offered to help her, I was in no position to really give away any money, I still lived at my parents, the holidays were around the corner, I had school to pay for and the general bills of life. I could have offered her some insight into finance managing, offer her an ear to listen to her, instead I put myself and our relationship in jeopardy because I offered.

You do not have to offer help where it is not needed or asked for. You can even decline if you're not in a position to aid. If you do not love and respect yourself you are not in a position to love and respect anyone else, because all that love that you could be using towards building yourself up is being spent on others.

Part III

Physical Being

Look at your body, right now, look at all the wrinkles surrounding your face, the love handles that you've never loved, the tummy that just won't tuck and that hideous mole you try to cover up with make-up. Look at all the things about your physical being that make you feel unnerved and unbalanced. Trace your finger around your flaws close your eyes, you still see them, you know why? You spend so much time trying to hide those flaws that they become imprinted in your mental picture. What if I was to tell you, you are perfect? Would you believe me? Chances are you would go through the things you hate about your body first and wouldn't believe me. Our bodies are material, they are what we can grasp with our hands and they are the world's first impression of you. You don't need to be conscious to understand this side of you, it's physical it is the manifestation of your spirit. If your body shows signs of distress it is the manifestation of your spirit, your spirit is signaling to you, I am not okay. While you do not need to be conscious to see your body, you need some level of consciousness to fix it. This is your vessel, your perfect, beautiful vessel, when you see flaws it is but a block in you that you need to work both outward and inward to correct to unblock. If you say I am a wonderful person, yet hate your body, or even one thing about it, it means that your soul does not feel wonderful. While we are here on earth we are contained in this physicality, so it is up to you to love it. If you say I hate this or I cannot stand that you are taking the mere physical essence of you and transitioning that hate within, once again the universe is going to respond to that and say, "oh you don't like that acne, here's some more." The first step in consciousness is learning to love every little flaw on our outward appearance as well as loving others flaws and transforming them from flaws to beauty marks, signs of the peaceful warrior waging a war against the conformity and control of society.

Beginning at a young age you are imprinted with labels, ugly, pretty, fat, skinny, good, bad. These labels carry throughout your life, popular, loner, rebel and stoner. We give everything a label at face value and if you allow yourself to be defined by all these labels you too will always be condemned to that label. When you see others you will contain them in a box with labels, you will always be looking at the label and not at the person, even if that person is you. If you say "I am ugly" you will live a life never feeling beautiful, your soul, being held within that ugly box you call a body, will always suffer and resent itself. Your self-confidence will lower and you will not be able to say what's on your mind, you will let people take advantage of you because you don't deserve anything and you will ultimately attract those alike you or those who will take advantage of you, only perpetuating your self-loathing. In the opposite respect if you label yourself with a label that says "I am pretty" you will live a life controlled by "beauty" how others view it, how you view it, you will chase the dream of being perfect in the world's eyes, not your own. You will vastly increase your ego and the bigger they are, the harder they fall. When you say I am the best and someone comes along and says no you are not, you will fall so far that your wounds from the fall can last a lifetime.

Imagine your body is always slick and wet; no labels can ever stick to you. You do not bind yourself by your chains and more importantly you refuse others to bind you. If you learn the homeostasis of humility and integrity your body will benefit, because it is that outward appearance that affects everything else that is composed of you. This is not to say health is not important. When I first started to fiddle with the realm of consciousness a reaction of mine was, "oh ok, this is only my physical self, I will continue on, but this weak vessel will wither and die, what is the use of preserving anything or not taking full advantage of this body." I look back at how unloving I was to my precious perfect vessel and it pains my heart. I have let it become so unhealthy that instead of a ship to carry me along my journey it had become like a cell to keep me confined in the little space I lived in.

You must love and respect your body; your physical being is the one that will take you through this imperative journey, while it can withstand vast amounts of destruction and repair itself it was not given to you to destroy but to use like training wheels until you are ready for a life without it. I believe in reincarnation and believe our bodies were meant to pursue what we needed to prior to being unified with our true selves, our true incarnations and our spirits. It is why an addiction that is affecting your physical body is what I believe holds us back from pursuing ourselves; it blocks our path to ascension. The addiction is not just of drug addictions, but food, work, friends; I even had an addiction to dreaming and I wanted to be in the world I could create so much more than this world. As time has passed I now realize how much influence I have at creating this world! A wise woman has told me that before we can get to be up there, we must live this life here. We are put on earth for a reason, in time we are all meant to ascend, but while we are here we are meant to live this life, experience THIS life. You should never over indulge it or deny it its necessities.

Recall how I perceive the four parts of you, all like separate people, well each one has a voice, the mind's voice is very loud, sometimes obnoxious and primarily guided by ego, your body is the shy child hiding in the back of the room, fearful to ever raise its hand. Your mind will continuously answer for your body and say, I know the answer, but the mind is not always right and if you do not allow your body the chance to speak and feel comfortable to speak your body will always be that shy voice. How do you listen to a person that never speaks up? Pay attention to their BODY language. If your butt is sore and you've been sitting all day, what is your body telling you? If your stomach hurts and you are doing the latest diet fad what is she saying? If your eyes are burning and you're yawning? We pay so much attention to the annoying kid in the front of the class that your energy is depleted when you think about your body you naturally assume there isn't any way to tell what my body wants versus my mind because they are one in the same, when your mind may want to go out and party, but your body is still recuperating from last night, your mind normally wins over because it has such a strong voice that if you do not concede to its desires you have to listen to it whine and whine and whine about how it's not getting it's way. "Why aren't you out partying, it's a weekend night? Do you really have to sit here another night and ignore the outside world?"

Your mind is a bully it tells your body, "shut up, you're not good enough to speak, you haven't gotten us anywhere." Your body, because it has been conditioned to say, "Yes, I'm not good enough," agrees with whatever the mind says and allows your mind to push it wherever it wants it to go. Look out for the signs your body says to you and acknowledge them and respect them, put your mind in time out and learn to love your body without limitation. Don't say, I would love myself if I was 20 pounds lighter, that is your mind talking. If you walk up a flight of stairs and get light headed or can't breathe that is your body saying, "ok I need help and you aren't treating me right and please exercise me more so that I do not suffer with this simple act." A great example in my life is my love of red licorice. Around seven or eight it was discovered that I had horrible reactions to anything containing red dye in it, what a bummer, if you look at almost anything red today it all has red dye, well when I consume it I tend to throw up a lot and well let's just say the other end isn't too happy either. I had always loved the taste of red licorice, even now my mouth waters, but my body has always been saying, "I can't eat that it makes me sick." My mind fights and says, "Yes you can, just a few won't hurt," for a long time I allowed my mind to win, to overrule my body and who in the end suffered? My body! My mind didn't need licorice it just wanted it, I've learned to block out every insistent plea of my mind and attempted to allow my body to freely express what she wants. In turn, I notice a great change in her.

Addictions are another area our bodies tend to lose the fight in, our minds say "I need this," and we do it and then who gets to go through withdrawals? Our bodies. I have had many conscious people use their consciousness as an excuse for addiction; even I have used it as an excuse. "Drinking helps me become more open, lowers my inhibitions and I perceive others easier. Smoking pot gives me that divine insight, gives me my muse. Cigarettes calm me down when I feel over stimulated by energy. Acid gives me the instant jump to the other world where I can commune with my soul." I don't disagree with these thoughts however, I do believe that when you consume something to aid with whatever you may be facing you open a gate, drugs are like a magical key that open any door. So who installed these gates and doorways to keep you out? In some facets I believe we have installed them, in others I believe our higher selves, our spirit guides, our guardians and the Divine Source has. When you steal a key to get through a gate and open it, it's like looking up the cheat codes to a game, so you beat the game, but do you have the integrity to look back and say you did it honestly? You have all the keys within yourself; you can open any door all by yourself. It will take work to get the door open, you may have to circle through your key ring a couple thousand times, but it is completely possible for you to achieve this without a forged key. You do not need an outside person or force to help you on your journey, if you chose to use someone or thing to gain entry to the gates on your journey it becomes their journey, the drugs journey. You cheat yourself because you're cheating your way through each obstacle that was placed in your path for a reason. We are all exactly where we are meant to be.

I've had many times where I get frustrated because I have such a strong empathic ability, but it seems all my other abilities are locked behind gates I have yet been able to open. When I have taken hallucinogens the gates open, I see what I have been missing and I want it more. If you're taking any form of physical alteration to open a gate within you as soon as you see what you've been missing you want it even more, you pursue it and most often through the same way you did before. When you get kicked back behind the gate and it shuts, your emotions churn, you're back in this stupid world you don't want to be a part of anymore, you want the world you saw. So you chase the high again and again, always needing a stronger substance to attain what you once had. Drugs lead to unconsciousness, where you allow others to control you, your energy and your vibrations, while unconsciously doing the same to others. We obtain highs from all sorts of outside forces, we never really know that we are numbing ourselves, unless we are aware of whom we are.

It is all possible within your own hands; you are the image of perfection, so how could you even possibly think for a second that the gate you unlock through your own will would be worse than the one you unlock through someone or something else? Your keys are yours for a reason, they unlock your perfection and while many have yet to go through any of their gates, the paradise is always there, awaiting you.

There is another way of cheating that comes not from a substance, but people. So you see a person and they used one method to get that gate to open. You see their gates open and you catch a glimpse of their paradise so you look at your gate and say "open sesame" but the gates don't open and you get frustrated because the gates opened for them, so why not you? A gate opener for me is music, I love beautiful chants, drums, singing bowls, bellsand opera, from the sound I ascend and I feel the emotion in every chord struck every note sung, for me it is one of my keys. If someone says "ok, she opened her gate with these singing bowl meditation's, so I am going to go and I will obtain that peace that she has." The person goes and it has the adverse reaction because instead of music being a key for them they really flourish when they are able to teach, so until they find this out about themselves their gate will remain closed. They may stand their screaming "open sesame" until their ears bleed, but that's not going to change how their physical body interacts with its surroundings. You have to be open to experimentation of the world. Go to a painting class, dance class, church, teach something to others and find out what your hobbies and passions are, because they are gate openers in the physical realm. If you have to coarse the drive to attend something, chances are it doesn't resonate with your soul and you just aren't meant to pursue it. Perhaps some nights you have this overwhelming passion to pursue something and other nights not so much. Be sure to honor yourself, honor your passions, whenever and wherever these may be. If you are in a library and feel like being loud honor that, follow your heart with freedom!

The physical world is illusion. What we perceive to be our senses are all illusions tying us to this realm of fiction. It is only real to us now because we are waiting for the curtain to lift. We are all so tethered to this world that often times, because it is the only thing that we can grasp through sight, sound, touch, smell and speech, we only understand this world. We refuse to connect with the Higher Sources, because we cannot grasp the Higher Source, we cannot study it or scientifically prove it. You can't study consciousness, but you can say, oh my body hurts, oh I see that bird, or that pie smells like apple cinnamon. We have conditioned our brains to interpret the physical world as the true world we belong to. This conditioning begins at birth, when we are held to certain standards, to excel, in this physical world. Not to think outside the box, because the box is all we have ever conditioned to believe that that is what is real. Reality is much deeper than the context society gives it. It is not simply the being that it explores; reality is the thoughts, the spirit and the feelings, just because we cannot measure these aspects does not mean that they are not in existence. We use the term "heartbreak" because when something happens that your emotions are so strongly tied to and it's an adverse action to what you desired your heart literally feels like its breaking.

We cannot measure this (yet) and say, your heart just broke 35%, not too bad, you can't complain, I've had my heart break 85%, this is nothing compared to that. Science in relation to consciousness can be a beautiful friend or a cold enemy. It seems as though when dealing with the infinite possibilities that science relates to the world seems so vast and endless, but the constraints that it puts on things are at the very same time so definite that people see no other option than to follow it. We can go past our perceptions and when we start to un-layer ourselves with all the masks of perception, much like we would an onion, we peel skin by skin; first easy, then harder and harder, we reach this tiny little seed of some sort, this little piece of us. We can stop there and say, wow, we only have this little piece of ourselves. But we also have that space that was once around us that the layers used to occupy and when that space is no longer occupied by the layers it is occupied by light; light that can reach you to your core now that you no longer have the layers, or masks, protecting you. In the physical we can say ok, my first layer is my clothes, my make-up and my outward appearance. Then, it is my outward demeanor, how do I interact with every living creature. Next, you say ok, my skin, past your skin is your internal demeanor, how do you secretly act towards others and yourself? As we go deeper and deeper into peeling off the layers it gets harder and harder, yet, the little piece that is left can be a beautiful piece but we never see it until we have removed all masks.

Our clothes that we put on, something as simple as clothes, has taught us all subconsciously to be shameful of our bodies. The stereotypes fitted around those who enjoy being naked or who wear fewer clothes than most are typically negative however, we were born into this world naked and I believe when we leave this world we will be naked. Nakedness is a beautiful natural part of us. By covering our bodies we resort to societies claims that the human body is a horrible thing, it's ugly and it's not acceptable. I ponder a lot on the story in Genesis about Adam and Eve. They did not run and cover their bodies when they were in union with God; they covered their bodies only when they became shameful of them. God created our beautiful bodies and we should not be in fear of them. No different than we should be fearful of sex. Union between another during this act is enhanced when you both have union with God. We have cast God out of the bedroom, but why? We have allowed our society to manipulate the grace and beauty both in sex and nakedness to be negative and associated with negative thoughts. The divine experience of sexual intercourse has taken on this evil perception. When we deny parts of our existence we suppress it, turn it into a cold and dark thing it grows and becomes too large and scary to handle. I think our societies lack of perceiving sex as beautiful has contributed to demoralization in the bedroom as well as a hidden nature that brings brutality into sexual intercourse. By denying ourselves acceptance to feel pleasure and share that pleasure with another we have taken our aggression towards that denial out on others and ourselves. Think of the sexual revolution of the 60's, you had so many repressed youth that realized they liked sex, they liked drugs, among other things and because they had been so controlled and suppressed you had this massive explosion of sex, drugs and rock and roll. This event wasn't about bringing peace to the world; it was about being free in their own skins as well as the society they lived in.

It is very intriguing to see how different religions and cultures approach sexuality and then what you see in the society as a result. In America you have high number of rapes, of murder, but what do we do? We desensitize our society to violence then suppress our natural curiosity of our bodies and our natural sexual nature. We have taken God out of sex and replaced Him with an evil dark force, brainwashing our youth that sex is dirty, evil and shameful, but we let them watch movies and play video games saturated with violence. From culture to culture you see massively diverse outcomes based upon their social acceptance of sex. This spans into homophobia, hate crimes, rapes and other instances where people are the victim of this beautiful gift being demolished. Certain religions go as far as female castration to ensure the female receives no pleasure in sex. If our Supreme Divine Source gave us our bodies I am sure He knew exactly what He was putting where, I don't believe this was meant to be removed. Even in cases where men, though so prevalent, are circumcised this act leads to men having to thrust faster and harder in order to ejaculate, often times not as pleasurable to a woman as an uncircumcised males slow, deep thrusts, that allows both the pleasure that God has given to us. Some cultures openly embrace female pleasure even suggesting that they learn their bodies, masturbate and get piercings to increase sexual pleasure, where this openness is encouraged you see education rooted in sex, more awareness as to what is occurring to one's body. Matriarchal societies rate amongst the lowest numbers for rape, homicide, suicide, burglaries, just to name a few. The acceptance of sexual beauty and love for the pleasure of the other liberates those involved and becomes a divine journey where two become one with The Source. Somehow, this act of love and passion has become dirty, secretive and about self-gratification.

Never underestimate the strength and beauty of your physical being. When you look in the mirror recognize that this is your soul's projection of how they feel and see themselves. You're a perfect being created in the image of perfection, never question it, don't let it go to your head, because we are all perfect. We need not to explain why or figure out how, we just are. Say "I am." Repeat it as many times as you need to believe it. "I am. I am perfect. I am light. I am beautiful." Something that I have been doing as my new bedtime ritual in order to grow the love and honor to myself I open a window and say a prayer, or manifestation while burning sage and cleansing myself, for myself. I envision that the prayer is being carried to my higher self and she appreciates the love I am showing her, I envision it is carried beyond to my Father and Mother. I have found that it gives me the peace for the night and it helps me to awake ready and rejuvenated in the morning. Find your own way of worshipping you, loving yourself and seeing your true beauty for what it is, not what it should be according to society. Love yourself.

Grounding

I have been ever exploring the world of me as well as that connection between myself and others. A couple weeks ago I went through a week where I was constantly out of body; it scared me, not because it was happening, but because I had very little control over it. I could feel myself floating, floating away. I have been practicing Kundalini Yoga, which is a practice that taps into the energy of the Kundalini which hides at the base of your spine, the base of the Tree of Life. This has opened up many things for me, amazing things. I have begun another face lift on the curtain. While the curtain is lifting- and quite quickly! I must balance myself in order to sustain growth. If I were to all of a sudden shoot up to the top, or the curtain were to completely lift, I wouldn't be able to control myself and I wouldn't experience this reality to the fullness of what I need to, while I am here. My guru has said many things on this, about how precious earth is, but more importantly how important it is to experience all that we have to in the present. She teases me quite often, knowing that my favorite place to be is anywhere but earth. I love floating and journeying and through practices have begun to harness the ability to float between worlds whenever I please. While I am still in the process of being able to do so easily I have come to believe that we also are in need of a strong ability to ground. I was so eager to rush straight to the top I never paid attention to how to balance myself and slowly increase my awareness instead, like most things in my life; I jumped in head first and eager. It has never been more apparent than recently, especially with the practice of Kundalini, that I need to find a way to ground. When I first began seeking that jump I would have intense moments of driving in the car after all my events to where I was somewhere in between where I journeyed and this reality. I wouldn't always know where I was, just knew that I wasn't here. It got to the point that almost the second I would get behind the wheel I would begin to float, because my car had become my oasis, my rocket ship. I have really sought out keeping myself grounded when needed and harnessing that ability to ground while I harness the ability to float.

I have found that the best things that help me to ground are things that envelope me in the physical world: cooking, cleaning, working out, and hanging out with friends and family, anything that requires interacting with my body. I do not believe that grounding should be a way to clutch to this reality, just as floating shouldn't be used to clutch you to the spiritual realm. There is a fine balance in all to keep you fluidly moving towards the end goal of ascension.

Part IV

Emotional Whore

Your emotions are like a prostitute. It may sound funny and that is the way to approach them. In a very light manner. You cannot see your emotional body getting upset and get upset with it and say, "why are you acting that way?!" You will find that she often calls most of the shots, you are the John and though you may pay and pay you may only get so much or may get a little too much from her. You feel in control because you are the one paying, but she is the one that says "yes you can pay." Imagine you see an ex who you have written off and sent along their own journey and you have gone on yours, it's been years since you've seen them, yet, when you see the new beau or belle on their arm your heart breaks. Your emotional body cries and throws a tantrum, you used to be that guy or garland you used to sparkle in their eyes. While she is very unpredictable she has a high ego, your emotional self will smile politely, pretend everything is fine and even ask questions that she doesn't care about. When you go home it is on your mind, your emotional self keeps reminding you. She has a very tactful way about keeping your mind preoccupied and under one guise or another. She will remind you only of the happy memories with your ex and she will say, you blew it, you ruined it.

How do you keep her under control? You learn how she works, she will have a habit of not facing the real problem and only reacting to the parts she wants to. So why did she get so hurt with the bump in of your ex? She is very clearly listing a need of hers, she wants a relationship. When you only see the good your emotional self is saying, "This is what I want." She sees that in your ex and projects her needs onto him. As you face your emotional body and really force her to look at herself you can go through your emotions one by one, it is a strong belief of mine that all emotions derive from two places, love or fear.

Love is patient, love is kind. It does not envy, it does not boast, it is not proud. It is not self-seeking, it is not easily angered, it keeps no record of wrongs. Love does not delight in evil but rejoices with the truth. It always protects, always trusts, always hopes, always perseveres. *(1 Corinthians 14:4-7)*

This passage is the true meaning of love, one of the best ways to describe love. We come to this understanding that love hurts, love is painful, truly, love is the only thing in this world that isn't painful. I believe that there is great importance in striving to achieve this interaction of love in all facets in life, from your mate to your annoying neighbor. When we achieve this level of love towards all we receive this love back from all, for it may not be apparent that your annoying neighbor is sending you love, but you will receive this gift from them in one way or another. By acting out in love in everything you do and not just saying that you do this, but allowing love to encompass your entire being, we interact constantly with God. The best way to interact with God is through acts of love. He smiles when He sees how we can love another piece of Him, love another piece of ourselves. All you need is love!

The worst thing I believe in this world is fear. It is the polar opposite of love and it is that which holds you back from anything you haven't pursued. Everything negative manifests from fear. When you are jealous you are fearful that someone has something you want. Angry, you are afraid that people will see your weakness and you want to show them how tough you are. The state of depression is the deepest part of fear you can reach. When you are depressed you see life through a clouded lens, everything you see is covered by fear. You are so rooted in fear that you cannot even fathom the state of happiness, you feel it is not a choice. When it comes to my emotions I am an extremist, so when I get sad it's not just a little sad, it overwhelms me and the only thing I can see is the misery plaguing my existence. This is something that I have learned to control only by forcing myself to look at things in the light. When you look at things in the dark you can't always make out what they may be. When you were a child you may even had looked around your room at night and seen everything as a monster, you may have projected all your fears onto all of your possessions. If you switched on the light you could see that it was just a stuffed animal, a coat hanger, or so forth.

The hardest thing about facing your fears is coming to the realization that you CHOOSE to be fearful and have fear based intentions. This is typically not a conscious choice, you don't say, "hey I'm going to be afraid of her so I am going to punch her in the face to show her how strong I am," or "hey he is going to get into a relationship with that girl so I'm going to go sleep with this guy to make sure that I am not the one 'left behind." Rather every time something bad has happened to you the experience gives you a small concrete block. You lay this block down, then another, another, until you have formed a fortress of fear that you live in. The ego is the builder and the blocks are all different fears. When someone knocks on your wall you say "go away, that block that you just knocked on is too painful." Even when the people trying to get in, trying to see us knock on a block that brings up sensitive emotions their intent is not to necessarily hurt you, they don't know that what they just said or did necessarily would bring you pain, but we take that pain and attach it right to the person. So you have people in your life that you associate with each pain until you have barricaded yourself alone away from the world in this dark fortress. You can choose to take away a block, you can let a little bit of light in and quit living in the darkness. When you see how good the light is it will become easier and easier to take down another block. Then what do you do with the blocks? Do you carry them around so your load is always heavy, just in case one day you need them? No, if you have made the choice to free yourself you need to discard that brick, just give it back to the earth.

The earth is like a balanced mother, she will discipline if you are seeking for trouble and will allow you to seek her out for comfort. Whenever I feel overwhelmed it is her bosom I turn to, I close my eyes and picture roots attaching me to her, I see her light energy flowing into me. She tells me, "here child, lay your burdens down, it will make the trip easier," and she welcomes my sorrows with open arms as she restores my joy. To a certain extent I am being contradictory; I say seek within for happiness, but then say I give my burdens to the earth. As with any problem it is ok to seek external input rather than internal. We have all the answers imprinted within, yet we have lost the connection to ourselves, to our internal guide and teacher so that, we don't always know exactly what to do. In any problem, I would rather seek help from the earth then someone else, because the earth doesn't have the intention of hurting you, but she does hold you accountable.

Someone else may see your weakness and when you ask them for help use it to their advantage to gain some kind of leverage over you. I use the earth to unload. Gaia is the only one strong enough to carry the weight of the world. If we are quiet enough she speaks, if we have the patience and reverence for her to listen.

I find it quite perplexing that the most common people that I know that have the biggest disconnection from the earth and least amount of love towards the earth are monotheists (this is not to say that I don't know variety from each group or that all of them are this way). The reason this is so perplexing for me is because, if you believe in one creator and you believe He, Her, or It created all, all of us, the earth, the animals, all life, then how can you disrespect such a gift? This is our earth and we must not only be diligent about keeping her healthy, but we also must remember our deep connections to the earth. I find it very interesting to go through cultures and civilizations and watch where we disconnected from reverence and common respect for our brothers, sisters and Mother. As you watch progression from Native Peoples (worldwide not just in Americas) to colonization you watch how we have all disconnected. The most impressive thing for me is the simple act of time keeping. Pyramids worldwide were created by supposed "primitive people" or "extraterrestrial beings," yet the establishment of the pyramids and other ancient architectural structures was not just some idea, let's build a tomb for the pharaoh who will be dead before we finish, or lets place it here just by chance. These structures are geographically placed and aligned to the stars, to the earth. It is completely redundant to assume that this was all by chance, that some sort of ironic event happened, worldwide that all these people just so happened to place these structures to align with everything so perfectly. In Hunbatz Men's book, <u>8 Calendars of the Maya,</u> he speaks of the Maya's direct connection to timekeeping. That everything was dictated in life in accordance to time, to ensure that the civilization was sustained and continued to flourish. They synched their calendars all to align with the time of the moon's 28 day cycle, their pyramids geographically placed to align with solstices and equinox's to stay connected in their daily life to the earth and the cosmos, connecting our mother and father by us. Their connection, I believe, is the foundation of why they were so prosperous and had love based intents throughout their daily lives. As we began through history to carve away at this connection I believe something happened to our emotional beings. We began drifting from our truly connected intuitive natures and more inclined to worldly desires and pursuits; less trusting to what we feel and more intent on finding answers from others; less of a connection and empathic nature towards others.

I take great note of those in my life that are more rooted to worldly pursuits and have less of an intuitive nature and are more inclined to suffer from severe depression, loneliness and social disconnection, leaving one to bury their head in the sand further. I find that this typically results from a strong connection to technology and anti-social activities. The more connected to other people we are the higher quality of life I find. I believe this to be because we search for that balance and the world is balanced based on our actions, when we connect to others, the cosmos and earth find a beautiful balance resting on us. We in turn, rest on them.

Gander through history, European civilizations really began to colonize and expand. I have many different theories on why they lost their connection, but the main force behind their negative pursuits throughout the world was control. Religion and land became a tool for their control. As expansion of the Roman Empire spread it began to dominate and alter religious or spiritual sects. From what I have studied in early religions they had very esoteric concepts and beliefs. Early churches did not consist of thousands of people gathering as we see today, they were held in private homes and spaces with small gatherings. These ideas were not always recorded in stone, often times they were spread verbally, for few knew how to write or read. This transference of ideas and philosophies could have contributed to a great amount of manipulation. Remember none of us are above fleshy pursuits. Picture it this way, the father of a household hears of these sacred teachings and adds some minor details to this knowledge to keep his household in his possession. His children grow and spread these beliefs, adding their own little details to the philosophies, possibly forgetting some of the original beliefs. This spreads and becomes further and further away from what was truth in the first place. Then you have the government that sees their control over their people begin to slip away, because the people now follow one Source and no longer worship their rulers. So the government concocts this plan to give their people what they want while subtly taking control, instead of causing distress and a massive uproar in their land. They build churches and temples for what their citizens want to believe, and then put literate people that they can control in power over these buildings and the citizens flock to the temples under the guise they are following their beliefs, yet in unknowing loyalty to their government. The government now has the autonomy to add things to the teachings to keep their power of control over the people.

Another manipulation could be that due to esoteric beliefs being eradicated, the writers and teachers began coding their messages in the teachings. So what seems like an innocent passage to the government are beliefs that have to be read in a certain light to understand.

The manipulation of texts and history is a two way street. Even people in power seeking to keep that control could have still been acting in what they felt was the best manner. It is similar to the way science fiction often depicts robots. That the robots turn on the humans to protect them, because humans cannot take care of themselves properly. The same way could be for people in positions of power, seeking to keep control in order to protect us from ourselves. This ultimately takes away our freewill. When we are lied to, to convince us to make the right decision we base it on false advertising and truly aren't able to make the decision that is most educated and in our best interests...according to us.

Understanding Vibrations and Energy

In the beginning there was sound and the sound was with God and the sound was God. *(John 1:1)*. These words are words that ring deep within my soul. Throughout cultures, civilizations and history you hear how important sound is. The ironic thing is how intertwined religious beliefs are, yet we say they are so different. In Hindu philosophy it is said that everything came from the sound OHM (AUM in some variations). We have Gregorian Chants in the Catholic belief, Gospel Music in many Christian Churches, Satanic philosophy claims that certain frequencies of sound (pay attention, not words, but sound) are ways to seep messages into the brain for mind control, many Native American Tribes use sound- chants, drumming, music- for their rituals. Sound healing is a prevalent belief, theorizing that "spontaneous healing" is possible through sound. Look all throughout religious cultures, sound is one of the most important piece of every religion Modern day cymatics studies raise many questions as to whether or not everything stems from sound. If you take salt and pour it on a speaker and play certain frequencies you will see geometric patterns forming (think sacred geometry) and as you change the frequencies the patterns change as well, but when you change it back to the original frequencies the pattern returns to the original pattern. The human body in the microcosmic sense follows a pattern, observe the cells that grow and make up larger cells that make up DNA, that continue to form the body; in the macrocosmic sense the Universe follows patterns, spirals that resemble some sort of DNA kind of structure. This is too precise to be coincidence. Patterns flow throughout all life. So if sound is able to influence patterns in just the simple setting of an amp and salt then why wouldn't it be able to affect us on a larger scale? If you play a frequency that matches some sort of matters frequency you can bring it to destruction, this is how glass shatters. Sound is vibration, so everything thus could possibly come from vibration?

Everything vibrates at a certain frequency; from us, human beings, to the universe, to the inanimate objects such as cars. Material items tend to vibrate in balance and harmoniously with each other while living beings are constantly fluctuating and interacting with the vibration patterns of everything that surrounds them. While certain items can retain energy and dispense it, we as humans along with the animals have a quite unique gift to harness energy and interact with other living organism through the energy we expel.

Have you ever noticed you walk into a room and feel that there is something wrong about the room? Like you knew that everyone there was just talking about you. Chances are they were. Our sixth sense is rooted in both our solar plexus (giving you that gut feeling when something is wrong, or those butterflies when you harmonize your frequency with another being) and our third eye (what most perceive as the sixth sense, the ability to see premonitions or paranormal entities, or anything of that matter). I have always known that I have a dominant empathic sense of others, I feel more than I am able to see, hear, or smell (yes smell!). I don't know why, but I always assumed that my heart chakra was constantly opened; it's why it struck me as odd when a person who has the gift of hearing people's frequencies told me that my solar plexus was wide open. It completely made sense! Of course!

I knew all the chakras and what they did just a lot of books tell you that the heart is what interact with emotions so divinely. I never even thought about my solar plexus, but it made sense seeing as how sensitive that area of my body has always been. Premonitions also come to me quite frequently. Ever since I was young I had dreams of the future, but more recently (I believe as a result of how my dedication and focus has changed) I have been able to have these visions in a waking state. Sometimes they are quite clear messages other times they only become clear in meaning after the event has already transpired.

I made a big mistake early on in life. I saw all my gifts as petty and wanted something more. I thought how stupid, all I can do is feel others emotions and I can't even control it to where I know what I am feeling apart from others. I resented it greatly and the small cherry on top of dreaming about the future didn't really help because they were all horrible dreams of ones I loved dying. When these began coming true I didn't know how to react and every time I had a dream of someone I loved I panicked! My mistake was closing off these gifts. I figured it would be easier to ignore it all then to try and utilize them.

It is important to protect your energy from both others and yourself. You are not meant to waste your own energy, just as others are not meant to take your energy. In both scenarios we have the freewill to steal energy just as we have the freewill to use our energy however we see fit. If you come to realize others tapping into your energy it is up to you to cut off their ability to do so. When it comes to your body and your energy you are in complete control. You chose what you want to allow happen to your entire being.

There are two types of energy vampires, the most common, the one who sucks our energy unconsciously and the other, who is aware that they are taking your energy.

The first type is so common because so many closed themselves off from being awake. When you combine this with the mind's need to hook others and your own attention you have masses walking the earth feeding off of stolen energy. There is an acquaintance of mine that is the first type. She is so in need of the pity of others to continue to gain her energy to live. Each time I talk to her she goes on and on about how horrible her life is. She rarely has anything good to say and though I have tried to steer her energy into other facets of her life she continues to wallow in her and others pity. It is hard for me to protect myself from her, because she is not consciously aware of the life she has created as well as the energy she is stealing from others. She is so clouded by her own pain that she cannot see the light in all of that darkness.

The second type is not as easy to spot unless you are aware of your own energy. This type has gone through life consciously manipulating others to gain control over their energy supplies. They are aware of what they are doing so are better at the ability of misguiding others to not recognize the negativity they are creating. I know a lady that falls into this second category. She is very much awake; I don't doubt it for a second. I feel that with the more clarity you gain you have more responsibility to share your gifts and insight into the world and spread peace and love versus seeing the imbalance in life and disrupting it further. When I became aware of the things she was stealing from me it was like a slow motion movie, I turned to her and looked her dead in the eye and it was as though the world stopped while I told her I wanted her to stop what she was doing. When I told her this her reaction sold the truth that she heard me. In that moment I caught a glimpse of her true self, I pushed her back sending out an energetic barrier between us and surrounded myself with light to protect myself. While I see her continuously seeking the energy of others I know that deep within she has a light that flickers through that darkness, an untapped potential.

When you find that people are subconsciously or consciously seeking to eat your energy up you must protect yourself from them! They are never going to reach their limit of energy because they are always so low on their own. They will never say, "Ok I have had my fill you can go now." People who mooch the energy off others will persistently feed off you until there is no energy to feed off of left, or until you protect yourself from them.

Practice different protection rituals for yourself. My mom, for instance, says the prayer of the Precious Blood of Jesus whenever she feels threatened, or like someone is tapping her energy. I do a number of things, I protect myself through meditations and sound as well as consciously send a message or force of love hurling into their body to wake them up to realize I am on to them.

After clearing up people in your life that steal your energy or cause you to become unbalanced it will become easier to clear up your belongings that are causing the same energy depletion. If you are surrounded by unpleasant things, especially on a consistent basis, you will pick up those vibrations and begin vibrating on that level. Say you have a necklace an ex gave you, your relationship ended horribly and every time you see the necklace you replay everything about the relationship in your mind. Even on a subconscious level this item interacts with your energy field and can manipulate you to still be consumed by the negative issues that you faced in the relationship. This can even act in the sense of a highly valued item, say you lost someone that you loved, you have a suit of theirs and every time you wear the suit or see the suit while you cannot part with it, it reminds you of the horrible day you lost them.

Every object you have has the ability to resonate into your energetic field and either disrupt or enhance your vibrations. For the more literal minded think of when you play music, if it is an angry song you find this energy inside of you that may be more negative, it is because the vibrations of the song is sending off a wave of energy, if your field is not strong enough then it can very well disrupt the happy feelings you were having before you played the song. A personal experience in my journey has been to audit everything I own, from my clothes to my random trinkets, to the posters on my walls. What inspires me? What envelopes me in peace and serenity? If I come home and have my sanctuary filled with clutter and things that don't allow me to feel secure then it pulls my frequency down. If you don't have a place that brings you joy and peace that you can spend time in, often then, you will find, that alone can be a big cause of disharmony in your life. With my hoarding tendencies I have to really limit myself on what will continuously bring me peace and serenity, so that when I retreat to my sanctuary I can really surrender myself and not have to worry about constantly keeping up my guard of protection. I have gone through the painful experience of parting ways with a lot of stuff. While the initial process felt impossible, little by little I find that I am becoming more motivated to part ways with my belongings and little by little I am at peace with this parting. The items I loved took up so much of my energy, I subconsciously gave a little piece of my energy to each item and each item had a different meaning. When I began to get rid of items that energy was restored to me and allowed me to redirect it towards my true passions and my true goals in life. Not only that, but now my sanctum is filled with more pleasant vibrations that interact and balance my own vibrations.

Empathically driven people have true risks of identity crisis, especially when dealing with vibrations. I personally, have a hard time shopping, because of the intense emotional waves I experience when I walk into a store. People are so aggravated and in a hurry that they ripple waves of negativity, when too many ripples hit you your energy it is overrun by these waves. It is an area that is completely possible to control I can control my emotions and I can allow myself to be protected from lower vibrating entities, but it is definitely something difficult to master. First, you must know that your own realm is completely yours; you are in control and can refuse to allow anyone else to control you. Then you must get to know yourself, know your feelings and know what is interacting with you and how you are going to handle it. This is an area where people become energy vampires.

. I have always been very aware and doing boundary checks on me with this area, because I am so in tuned with others I take precautions to ensure that I am not sucking from another's energy. If I all of a sudden feel great I look around and say am I feeling this or is this someone else's? It can work in the opposite respect, I frequently get other people's pains, I used to say, "I will take their pain away, because it will bring them peace and I can handle it." I went through years of excruciating pain, I didn't always consciously know I was taking on someone's pain, but because I had become so accustomed to taking on people's pains I became natural at this. I tend now to not take on someone's pain but instead envision them in light, everyone has their own darkness to deal with and I cannot take your darkness and expect you to be ok, because the hole that is creating it is still open for you. In that case I can fill my vessel with so much darkness and never heal anyone. I never help them because it is their burden to bear, just as I have mine and I will never be able to seal the hole within them. Then you have two people instead of one filled with darkness. I can, however, envision them manifesting love into their life which will help them fill the hole. I can expose all my light to the world and others may choose to follow it like a light house while I remain filled with my energy and light.

Relationships

Your relationships in this physical world are keys to gates to the spiritual realm. How you interact with every single creature is a direct reflection on how much light or darkness is held within your soul. The more you let the light out the more the light shines upon you and the harder it is to retain darkness.

Relationships are an aspect of all realms of you. You interact in all four areas so it is only appropriate to assume that everyone else does, you will however, deal with a lot of people who solely base their relationships in the physical world. Think about it, in so many ways we interact in the physical. Even though our physical body is what we tend to most criticize about ourselves. We create action with our bodies so when we show affection or fear we show it through our bodies, we hug, kiss, sexually connect, or in the latter, physically hurt people. The human touch is a miraculous thing, it can diffuse a ticking bomb or it could detonate it. When we touch someone who we are fighting with, even if it's in the slightest of ways our bodies feel that spark of passion and it ignites within us. Think of a time when you were in a heated debate and someone touched you to try and get your attention so you would hear their side, they just put their hand on your wrist or something simple and you reacted and said, "Don't touch me." They invaded your space and you did not welcome them in it and that is why you reacted. If someone is invited into your physical space you wouldn't have had the same reaction, you would feel them and that would calm you down. I respect touch so much more than I used to. We are deserving of a connection to other beings physically just as we are in the other areas. You may deserve, but it doesn't mean that you have the right to invade someone's physical boundaries without invitation, without consent. It's not to say you have to go around and ask people to kiss or hug them, but read their body as if you would your own, if they have their no trespassing sign up, don't trespass, respect their bounds as you want yours respected and leave it at that. If you feel that you need to share a physical connection with them, then ask. "Can I give you a hug?"

Relationships, for me are the hardest step of attaining consciousness, because you come to the realization that, no your spouse does not treat you the way you need to be treated. Your coworkers are emotionally draining and don't seem to respect you, you have friends who've never respected you. The list goes on and on, ultimately it is up to you to say, "I cannot continue to exert my precious energy on your negative emotions." You have to be the one that withdraws from the relationship. This can be done in small steps and is probably easier than taking on the entire load at once.

First, find people that are living the reality of happiness, that are vibrating at a high frequency and that do not need your energy reserves to thrive. When you surround yourself with uplifting people it is easier to recognize and detach from those who do not have your best interest in mind and who seek to make you as miserable as they are.

Then you look at your relationships at work, your work is exhausting you, your coworkers and boss only have the interest of money in mind and your wellbeing is being compromised there are two routes, you can attempt to draw your boundaries and let them know you are not interested in being walked all over anymore that you have your highest interest in mind and need an environment that welcomes them. If you find that that does not help then unfortunately it is time to leave. Always come from a place of love though, don't bark orders and expect it will change, love them and more importantly love you enough to say "I need this for me." Very simple, yet SO powerful! It doesn't have to be a battle for you to win the war, because the war is with yourself, with tapping into your true potential.

Moving past this you go to your more intimate relationships, your friends and family. As children we learn to honor thy mother and father, or whatever context you want to put it in, bottom line we learn to respect authority above all else, laws, police, elders. More often than not you find that truly you fear above respect, you do not learn respect through fear you learn it through love. As you get older you wonder why it's harder to maintain these relationships, it is because you grew up in fear. When fear is the only thing that bonds you to someone and that fear fades you no longer have any attachment to a person. Though it may be hard if your relationships, even those with people who you feel so close to, are built with fear, it is time to end them. You can attempt to tell them your boundaries, but you have to draw the line first, the universe is not going to say, okay what line do you want to draw. People do not wait for you to tell them how to treat you; they treat you how they grow accustomed to.

The best way I go about dealing with the stress of losing others is imaging the worst case scenario I say to myself, the worst thing is I will lose them. If I lose them then did they ever truly love me in the past? If they are not going to respect my boundaries then why on earth would I want them in my life? It is, I feel, the most painful part of consciousness, coming to terms with the loss of relationships and coming to grips that I was never loved by these people, I was just used. Usage can be more than physical. People WILL try to use you for your energy source. Consciously or subconsciously they will tap into your reserves to keep them feeling happy. You see, when people constantly vibrate in low frequencies they quickly burn off their energy. Ever heard the term it takes more muscles to frown then smile? Same is true when it comes to your energy. It requires more energy to remain negative; if someone depletes their energy it is natural for them to seek another source of energy. If your energy is easily acquired you become the next target.

You can be a very conscious person, very aware, but say you have a father that is constantly depressed, who constantly speaks of negative thoughts and reflects upon his past in a very sorrowful way. You love your father and feel that somehow you can help ease him out of this state. As time goes on you find yourself growing weaker and weaker when dealing with him. Out of love and compassion you see it as your duty to guide him out of this destructive lifestyle; however what is happening is he is gaining more and more energy from you to continue his downward spiral. Your love will not be enough to "save" anyone, even if you care about someone so much. The best thing you can do is withdraw that energy source, tell them why you are doing it. "I love you, but I cannot continue to support the way you live. I want to maintain my serenity and being around you and listening to horrible stories over and over again is not serene to me." This may seem harsh but you are only responsible for yourself, you cannot heal everyone, especially those who do not want to be healed (free will principle). In this scenario the worst case would probably be that they would commit suicide, you must overcome this fear to protect your life, because no one else will.

So you've come to the realization that you are in a marriage with someone you feel no connection to. You swore to love them until death, in front of God, you family, friends, them and yourself. You may understand that you can no longer go about being in a loveless marriage, but you swore, that is your word on the line. From a more secular view you may feel guilty, you may say that you swore this in front of God, how could you turn your back on him and just back down from a promise?

I have personally never been married, but I will draw from two different scenarios I have witnessed and express my thoughts on each and the conclusion.

First, let's call them Steve and Shelly. Now I don't know the exact events that had transpired in this marriage but I know enough. Being naturally empathic I have always had a great understanding of people, almost right off the bat I get that feeling of who is pursuing good in the world and who intends to do harm. When you become more aware and more conscious your interactions and abilities both with others and yourself grow exponentially. While Shelly and I have had our moments of tough times I know the kind heart she does have. She is very generous and too often I have noticed her fatiguing herself for others. Steve, while a generally good character, there has always been something off when I speak to him. I feel like a weasel even when I see him. I try to allow others the free will to make their own impressions and not intervene especially with matters of the heart. They had been married for 40 years! Both actively involved in a Christian religion they seemed like a perfect couple, if only you just hear their story and glance at them. However, Steve had been having an affair with someone very close to Shelly and even left her for the other woman. You could feel the pain when Shelly would walk by, though a smile always graced her face. I could tell that she was struggling with the same situation as my mom had, she didn't want to betray God or anyone else by ending the marriage, even after she had been treated so disrespectfully! He came back after a year of living with this other woman. She attempted to rekindle their relationship, only to face her fear and succumb that the relationship was no longer healthy for her or for their children.

The second couple, Mike and Ann, had been in a marriage that seemed doomed many times. Mike was always very self-conscious about sharing his all, about exposing himself and being vulnerable. I know that Ann was always pushing him to open up and reveal all the things he had been bottling up. They too were very Christian and Ann specifically refused to give up for that simple reason. After 15 years of being very unhappy and trying different avenues to get Mike to give up his stoic personality and open himself up, to get him to trust her, after Ann and their children had put up with years of abuse he finally broke down culminating with a death in his family. It broke him so much that all the shell had completely crumbled; there was only his true self left to see. Five years later they are now happily married, blissful and in love with each other more deeply than before.

Mike had always been afraid to show himself and Ann had always loved him she had put her own self on hold for 15 years! While I probably would not have the patience to wait that long, think about if Ann would have left him while waiting it possibly would have made him feel less trusting in the world.

There are different paths that we are all presented with in different scenarios all with different outcomes, people look to see the right or wrong answer, but truly each will help you grow. You do not know every possible outcome, but one thing is certain, you can grow from each outcome. When it comes to marriage I see it as a deep commitment, one that shouldn't be taken lightly. But if you've come to the point in your awakening where you feel that the marriage is only in store for more disaster and you are only staying in it because you feel guilty about leaving it, think of yourself. Does this person love you and respect you? Is this person going to be the person to help your life flourish and to grow with? Is this a person you can help flourish and grow with? If these answers are no, admit to yourself the worst case scenario, then ask if you are ready to face those fears. You should not stay in any kind of relationship that is putting your life and soul at risk. You are a beautiful person and should not be subjected to anything less than your best.

The Twin Flame Paradox

Too often I see spiritually conscious or aware people falling victim to the thing that we all fall victim to, love. This is not a bad thing in any way! Love is a beautiful exchange between two people, from the physical expression of love in sex to the burning sensation within your heart; love is a great thing to have! The simple act of loving another is super beneficial for you as well, if you truly are acting out love. I often think of Happy and wonder if I truly loved him, I wanted to control his world and he wanted to control mine, so was this love? Our relationship began with us under the belief that we were twin flames and I wonder if this was the reason we "loved" each other. If we felt obligated? I find that the idea of twin flames actually acts out our own fantasies of union to ourselves. When we seek that union it is like seeking light to fill the void, we try to find the brightest light to fill that hole inside of us. The brighter the light the better it feels, but it is still not our own light. Furthermore, when we use someone else's light to fill that void it's never going to feel as good as our own light. I don't know whether or not twin flames exist, but if they do exist I am firmly against the idea of you being able to reunite while still so empty. It is my belief that you would meet these people at a point in your life when you are already relying on your own light to fill that hole.

It has been months that have passed since I broke this world I lived in, since I began writing this crazy collection, since Happy and I parted ways. In the beginning I was a girl, hurt and filled with this great void, a great light (Happy) that I had known to fill a portion of that hole had left me and my hole and I was left with that sense of emptiness. As much as that point in my life hurt, it pushed me onto a path of self-exploration that I have yet to finish seeking. As I have evolved my collections have evolved with me, just as while you are reading I hope they have evolved with you and brought different things into your life. I set out in writing to disprove the twin flame ideology and to prove to the world that I could be one with myself. It was some of the greatest counseling I have ever commenced. It came from within, it was truth and this truth has become clearer and ever more present in my life through time.

My writing has taken on a life of its own. I seek not to guide it anywhere I simply write. I find that in depending on me for the first time in my life, in trusting in my wisdom I have become more whole, but I also feel a sense of never being completely whole in this world. I reach mile markers in my journey that I used to conceive as being a place I would feel completely whole and enlightened, but as I reach these points I feel like the visualization of wholeness has changed and evolved. I now feel such a greater sense of what it means to be whole and I severely question that that can be reached while living within a fleshy being. I feel that when I reach wholeness will be when I become unified with the source of all.

Enter Aqua Man (AM). I have had some great loves in my past, as much as I would like to say negative things about each one, they all helped me get to certain places in my life and ultimately I allowed their negative instances to affect me. I see that the only common thread any of them had was me. AM has come into my life at a point where that common thread has changed, I no longer feel victim to love and I feel such a sense of self that I no longer need the comforts of another's cage to help me feel honored. AM has brought a sense of disillusionment to my life, he has already taught me so much about myself, particularly in the facets that I try to "educate" others and his own love for self has taught me that I cannot teach anyone. I can simply open doors for them. He has sparked, for me, a new way of aiding others. I find it is a much easier way as well. I can lead these people and bring them to the doors, I can even open, but pushing someone through a door they may not be ready to walk through does no good. Instead this quiet validation of each person brings a much happier interaction into our life. People I find are more receptive to that calm presence versus trying to beat an idea into their head. There is something special in AM that resonates with a part of my soul, but it is not my basis to live, to thrive. I understand one day he may be gone, but I dwell in the presence and avoid questioning when that will be or how I can tie him to me. We have this friendly dance between us two, a dance that allows us each to live our separate lives, to be free and for times allows our paths to cross. Neither one of us seeks that control over the other, the control that I used to seek, that before I enjoyed being placed over me. It is the first time that I feel just simply at peace in this weird relational thing.

I have come to a place in my life that I believe AM has truly helped cultivate; he has allowed my truthfulness to break free. I feel such freedom with him; not only in physical, mental, spiritual and emotional pursuits but to freely say what I want to say without fear of repercussions. I feel that every relationship I have been in, romantic or not, I have tip toed around words and what was on my mind. I have allowed my fear of hurting others, of angering others, of challenging their beliefs to dictate what I say and don't say. I denied myself this beautiful way to express myself my entire life. I do believe that this has been made easier in my personal pursuits for growth and by other people, but AM showed me how free truth sets you. The fact that I could come to someone that I hadn't known too long and bring to him something that was on my mind and he not only responded in a welcoming fashioned but he continued to encourage a truthfulness in me. I never knew how attracted to truth I was. I have since set out to be truthful to those in my life that I feel I have wronged or feel that have wronged me. It is not out of a place of anger, hurt, or spite that I am determined to do this it just is time to cleanse and release. I unscrewed the lid and poured out on AM and he smiled and I went on my way to pour out onto everyone in my life, to right wrongs.

AM has initiated much more within me, being naturally guided by emotions I was taken by surprise when I felt something that I had never felt caused by any one person. I was sitting on AM's lap and we were looking at each other and as I often do I saw past his flesh and deep into his soul. I felt his sensational being and this caused a feeling I have never experienced in my life. I felt this burning sensation in my sacral chakra that built upward to my heart, when it reached my heart center it was as if that energy exploded. I got goose bumps all over my body and this calm presence of divine love. I wasn't prepared for this feeling at all, it nearly moved me to tears, but out of fear I held these tears back. The only thought in my very still mind was "oh shit," I didn't plan to fall for him, even more I hadn't ever experienced this feeling and feel as though I have never truly known romantic intimate love until this moment of my life. Until this moment when I believe him and I together became unified with God. As he spoke to me I was literally speechless, all I could say was "yeah." I am continuously surprised at the amount of faith the universe bestows upon me. To give me that gift of radiating love for another being, to allow it to surpass anything at that moment in time and most miraculously—continue to grow! I am so grateful!

I think it is important to count your blessings, not to push everyone in the glass half full view, but recognize and honor the universe and yourself for being gifted such a great experience, especially in times of stress when you feel down or disheartened, think of the last time you felt love—for that was a gift from our creator, the only gift in life that is worth anything and infinitely worth everything.

When I think of AM I place faith that our futures will continue to grow I leap into the unknown if that will be with or without him, but I know that at the very least I will walk away from my experience with AM with a more profound sense of truth, love and some of my best memories.

As for that whole fantasy world I don't place any expectations on anyone that they are my twin flame and further more believe that, that faith, in one another is one of the most damaging things in love. If I place so much belief in this one idea then you see two interactions. One, being that I have this expectation over another, that is nearly impossible to meet, that they are the one that has to live up to my crazy fantasy, if they shall fail then I have negative reactions, if it is in love you have no expectations, you come and go as you are. The second interaction you have is the person chasing their tail or rebelling against this, doing things just to "fail" or fall into compliance with this expectation, being untrue to their own nature.

I do love the aspect of that fantasy, that there is one specially made for you, one that is completely a part of you. This may be true, I don't quite know. I do feel a sense of this within myself though; that our longing to be unified with others is just our own expression of what we are missing in our life. When you release your fears and expectations in external forces you find this overwhelming love within, which brings forth a new sight in everything. Your radiating beauty fills the world around you and the world you touch; it is so amazing how much light being in love with you brings the world!

Part V

Mental Case

Your mental personality is the most comfortable; he says whatever comes to mind all the time. He is always speaking and will always let you know what he thinks. Sometimes we forget how to listen to him so he tells us things that keep our attention, like how your basketball team just won or the girl at the coffee shops name, little unimportant details that seem to be at the top of your attention. He tells you, look at this, look at that, incessantly. He is conditioned to what you will pay attention and like a child is starving to hold your attention so he will only bring up the things he knows he can get you to focus on. In the past few years I have noticed a great increase in my mental capacity; I frequently check in on myself and make notes on how I've changed. The perception I see with will certainly be different and as I continue my journey I know that it will get easier to focus on the things that truly matter in my mind; things that derive from my spirit.

I remember going to a buffet probably about three years ago, always having the feelings of others I have been accustomed to drowning out the emotional overload however, when I was sitting in the back with my friends I found a new thing that I couldn't quite comprehend until much later, I was hearing everyone's thoughts. It was bustling but what I was picking up on was not their physically spoken words. I heard much more than that. While at the time it was a new concept I noticed it happening more and more frequently I could hear people chattering about in their minds. I've found that the more I pay attention to this the more it overwhelms me. I feel and hear the thoughts as if they were my own. Similar to my precautions with emotions I use protection meditations as a way to keep from being bombarded with these thoughts.

I have tested many times the ability of telepathy and have found that more often than not I can send out a signal to someone that I know and have them respond to it. I could tell you many stories, but one of my fondest is when I was about 11 my uncle took me to California to visit my best friend, on our way out there he got a flat tire. I was so scared. This was before cell phones were so popular and there we sat about 3 am (can't quite remember the exact time now) when miles and miles away my mom awoke with this horrible sensation. When we called her in the morning at a gas station pay phone she said that she had been worrying so much over us and the exact time she woke up is when we got a flat. I have always had a close bond with my mom and I believe that in some way she knew I was scared and was responding to my distress signal in the only way she knew how.

Another of my accounts comes from a friend, that had gotten in a car wreck and just after it he said that he went to sleep and when he woke up he was over his body staring down at it. He believes that he was dead, just hovering there looking at himself, his phone began ringing and he knew he had to answer it. In a flash he was back inside his body with the phone in his hand; it was his mother. She had called because she had a bad feeling. However it works out cases like this or when you think of someone and bump into them aren't just coincidences, I believe his mom is so connected to him that she knew something was wrong with him. I personally think that this world and all of us are way too intelligently designed to just be full of coincidences. We are also way too connected to not have this natural ability. It is whether or not you pay attention to these instances to which determines if you will receive more. It is the most important warning I give when I say, Do not clod your mind eye. Our mind is the connection between spirit and body.

For me, more than even my emotions, my mind is the hardest thing to quiet. I have taken pleasure in more active meditating like yoga, belly dancing and even something like listening to singing bowls. If I have something to focus on with more intent it helps me to remain focused. I have cut TV out of my life with the exception to the occasional movie and I am a sucker for paranormal and metaphysical documentary style broadcasts. I don't watch the news because the only thing that is ever aired is stuff that just is negative. For every 20 bad things there is only one good thing. Remember, your mind is conditioned to point out things that keep your attention, if you constantly show your mind that negative things keep your attention he will show these to you every chance you get. If you preoccupy your mind with positive images and things then it will try to get your attention by pointing out positive things.

Reprogramming is hard, you can't just say, I am not going to watch TV anymore and I will throw out all the music that doesn't bring peace to my mind and I will stop hanging out with people who only speak negative things and expect it to be so easy. The second you try and cut one thing out your mind will be right there, "hey remember how funny it was when we watched that show where all they do is hurt each other? Hey remember that song you like so much about killing people? Hey I miss so and so who was always such a fun person to drink with." Your mind has a memory that makes it difficult to just start fresh, so, start small. Integrate positive images into your life, put a picture up of you smiling that you feel your best of, surround yourself in images that make you feel happy. Then go through your music, if you find it's just a bunch of junk that talks about partying and doing drugs start listening to music that invokes a positive message. Surround yourself with people who are upbeat and you share positive things with, if you have a bunch of friends that you just party with and those are the only people you hang out with it is time to at the very least, distance yourself from them. Remember this is YOUR life, you shouldn't feel guilty about wanting a positive change. I look at so many friends from my past and the common thread we shared was getting high and drunk with. When I stopped drinking and doing drugs I lost a lot of friends, it wasn't me who made the choice to lose them, they didn't want to be around me because I was no longer interested in the only thing we shared. Even now my mind is still a big obstacle. But as the saying goes, it is a terrible thing to waste. So slowly but surely I am learning to redirect the mass amounts of energy my mind has into more meaningful endeavors.

If you're not ready to make these changes then at the very least keep a journal, write down your goals, write down affirmations, when you wake up write down your dreams. Revisit past entries every so often and see how you have grown. When I look back at some of my affirmations it gives me more fuel for my future endeavors, when I see how much I've grown I know I am on the right path. I talk to each part of me daily and do check-in have to see how they are all doing. As I continue this growth it is being affirmed each second by being gifted with more energy and more life opportunities to challenge myself with.

Part VI

Spiritual Blessing

Perhaps the best entity out of the bunch is your spiritual embodiment. This is your true self, your higher self. Your perfect self. The spirit is not subject to opinions and is the source of your energy when you feel that you simply cannot continue on. People say "I feel the Holy Spirit moving through me," but I know that this feeling is attainable whenever you want it. I found this out one day lashing out saying, "HOW COME I DON'T FEEL THAT ALL THE TIME?!" In an instant I was overcome by that beautiful blissful feeling. More and more as I concentrate on finding this person that I have lost in my life, that I have forgotten I feel this overwhelming love and joy come to me and it restores me in every way. If you've ever felt pure bliss you know how beautiful it is, you don't need any words to describe just the feeling of love radiating through every cell of your body. I believe that we are here on earth to rekindle this single relationship. This is what it is all leading up to. To find your true self and let go of the chattering mind, the emotional baggage and the feeble body. Our bodies are temporary but our souls have eternal life and can break free from the suffering of this world.

Every time that you come from a place with love it is your spiritual self-acting. Our true selves have no ego; our spirits remember where we came from before and see the wrong that we have done, yet they show compassion and love to everything, including our earthly bodies. While this is our true self, we live in a world where hardly anyone realizes that they never commune with their true selves. We are under a deception of believing that the real us enjoys shiny cars, watching TV and eating fast food.

Our society has captivated the attention of our mind and told us what is good and bad. People who are spiritual in any way are seen as outcasts when truly those who live spiritual lives are the only ones who truly know who they are. When I say you are the one you have been waiting for, your waiting for the true you, your soul to reconnect to your physical body, I believe this is the journey we are making, to reconnect to your spiritual self.

Despite popular belief, religion is not the same thing as spiritual. You can be spiritual while being religious, but just because you're religious does not mean you're spiritual. I have struggled with this concept so much. Early in life raised Catholic in a Catholic school I was surrounded by all the "right ways" of doing things and many religions make the mistake of saying, "this is the only way." I was so unhappy following the conformity of religion and I saw that because I was suffering and depressed that it was only natural, that I was only carrying my cross. I believed that the "righteous path was hard" and it is, but being so devoted I wondered, if I believe in this benevolent God would he truly want me to suffer this way? Is this a test of his? Or am I just justifying my suffering that I am causing?

I'm not just calling Catholics out here, it's all religions and we are under the perception that "my religion is right, so I am going to condemn you, because only my religion is going to heaven." If you think this then you will be surrounded by very few people in heaven, when hell will be full of billions of souls, would your God truly want to see so many of his creations perish in a lake of fire? I suffered so much thinking constantly if I didn't run to the priest and tell him all my sins then I would certainly go to hell. I believe the concept of confession is so flawed in that, I don't think that if there was just one God he would send humans forth to be the judge for him, I don't believe that the priests have the right to say, "You're forgiven." I believe it is more important to seek out the ones you have wronged and ask for their forgiveness, even past that ask yourself to forgive you. If someone forgives you we all have a tendency to continue to carry the wrong we did. You wonder why the journey is so hard, it is because throughout life you pick up all sorts of junk, that you really don't need to carry and soon enough your load is so large that you feel you cannot go on. It is time to lay down the burdens, lay everything down that burdens you, carry on light and free of all that plagues you.

It also works in reverse, I went through a phase where I saw all religion as evil, well, they are not right I thought, so it must be wrong, all these people who are following this hypocrite life of loving others, but only if they are what you believe is right and condemning everyone else, are crazy because they are spreading this poisonous pain to everyone. It took me awhile to see that everyone has their separate paths; just because I don't need the comfort of religion doesn't mean that for someone it doesn't bring them a true sensation of peace and joy. For some, this is where they align with their soul. So when you see someone and try to enlighten them and bring them into a place of more light, just understand, while you may not believe it, they may not be ready to believe what you do, they may still need the training wheels of religion, in their next life they may be ready to take them off, but it is their free will to do what they wish, if it's what makes them happy, who are you to come along and crush that joy? Then, you are no better than the hypocrites.

How do you get to a point to where you are one with your soul? I believe that you need to go through the other areas of your life and when you are happy and healthy in all areas you will find more and more of your true self reunifying with your physical body. When people talk about twin flames I believe that it is our physical selves seeking to be unified with the other half of us. So your physical body tries to transform it into a sense they understand, another physical body. It is not to say that our spirits are not out there in another plane interacting with other souls, loving other souls. I believe even in the possibility that our souls may be married in some sort of way to others, creating a yin and yang effect, completely balancing and complimenting the other. I believe that when our physical bodies see the physical bodies of those we know in the spiritual plane they rejoice, it's what I believe is the spark in so many relationships, not just romantic, ones. I believe we are drawn to each other because that is what we are so comfortable with, we have seen their true selves and how beautiful they are so we want to find them, our physical body needs to transform that feeling of the soul into this world, needs to secure that feeling of connection and love that you share in a community of souls in the physical world. That is the only thing the body can understand, physical things that it can see, touch, taste, smell and hear. Anything that falls outside of the category is the mind or the spirits realm of understanding.

The soul understands everything and understands it all in light. It does not hate those that choose a lower path, it says "that is your choice, I see you and one day I know that you will come to the light, but not a second before you are ready." Like Namaste, to see the light in another and respect it. The soul loves regardless; it doesn't place impossible expectations on others because it knows that everyone has their own route and that everyone is capable of being full of light and love. It understands that it has grown through the years and has not always been able to be surrounded by light. It sees the beauty and perfection in every living creature and it doesn't blame or judge them, it understands that fear and hate solve nothing that the only way to help someone is by loving them.

Glamorized Spirituality

I believe one of the enticing things about spirituality is how sparkly it looks standing on the outside. I recall a time, which wasn't too long ago, where I would come across people who seemed to have this sense of knowing, this sense of inner peace. All I saw was the sparkle they put off, I didn't see their struggles or how they came to be standing in this glamorous spiritual light. I grew resentful, because I did not understand. It was the idea that they could have something that seemed unachievable to me. Pursuing spiritual peace in one way or another my entire life I thought that they were all just pretending or, worse, that they truly had this peace, as if it was just handed to them on a silver platter. I thought, how can you have that? I have tried to have that forever, you can't have that!

As I grew to know the various spiritual leaders in my life it became clearer how hard they had worked to get to this point. I saw more than a few of them at their most vulnerable, tears, yelling, upset, overwhelmed, fleshy. This struggle in them, as weird as it sounds, allowed me to find peace with my own struggles. I began seeing that we all struggle, we all have these moments that seem beyond our control and that the rollercoaster isn't just filled with the ups. The sparkle of spirituality didn't wear off; it just seemed to spread to my own life.

This is one of the reasons I believe I began writing. I felt frustrated with how easy it seemed to come to most and to me, the one thing I wanted so badly, to be unified with my Source, seemed to be so hard. Truly, everyone suffers these boulders that fall upon our paths. No one knows how deep the world cuts, especially when we have only ourselves and our

God to deal. Those thoughts of the lower vibration begin to sink in, begin to ring through our mind, you're a failure, you suck, you cannot ever achieve true spiritual bliss, true happiness.

Whatever spiritual bliss is, I promise, it is obtainable! No matter how many times you stub your toe, cut your feet, step on thorns, get dirt on your heels, keep walking, one day, you will be on the inside of that spiritual bubble and though it will be baffling at times at how someone could ever look up to you, look to your light, it will happen. When this does happen you will notice that people from all over old and new will gravitate to you, they subconsciously see the light you emit and want to follow it. Sometimes they recognize their attraction for what it is, they will understand that you have found that inner peace, other times they will not understand this attraction and will just turn to you as a sunflower turns toward the sun, following your light. Hold on to this feeling of light, of specialty, for there will also come a time when people begin to try to steal the light, kill the light, or stop your light from growing. Again this will be on a subconscious or conscious level. People may not want to hurt you, but they will try. Just because our intentions are pure doesn't mean that the outcome will be beneficial.

Spiritual Warfare

There is this force that because of our perception of reality we have little awareness over. Music, television, pop culture, clothes, drama, fear, pain and loneliness cloud our awareness. We allow this idea to influence our attention and we pay more attention to these external forces than to our true nature and our divine source. We place such a high value on material pursuits, but truly are only giving our precious energy and attention to things that truly don't matter! When it comes to drug or alcohol addictions we can clearly label people and say "oh they have a problem," but what of those that devote all their time and energy to TV, video games, work, shopping, or even another person. I have often played the role of super hero in other people's lives. From the small intervention to the larger consistent need for my support. I don't believe that it is bad to rely on others for support or to support another in their endeavors, we truly are communal beings and we seek that union and affection from one another. BUT where it can be damaging to a person is where it turns into a need. "In order to be happy I need you," or "In order to be happy I need you to need me." These are two principles many people fall victim to. The reasoning behind it is so easy and logical to someone that has never been equipped to be self-sufficient. I can easily say that due to my family history of having "abandonment issues" I fell quite nicely into the second category. I needed everyone to need me. I spent so much time fearful of ever needing another, fearful that if that became true then they would just leave me, just as so many close bonds in my past had. I never perceived myself as a victim, because it was my logic, that "I am stronger than this person that is why they NEED me." Truly, there is a beautiful vulnerability in being humble. Humility allows you to see things as they are and not judge yourself or another too harshly.

My spiritual journey certainly has humbled me. I have dealt with everything from people lashing out at me, to falling victim to my own fears and concerns. It is a dance and interaction with everything, that in order to be strong in our interactions, from ourselves we have to demonstrate humility, perseverance and love. There is something very scary about the world we are entering and that is evolving around and within us. Dualistically it is also something very exciting and wondrous. The time is NOW and if you are waiting for some spiritual leader or some sort of hidden sign that it is NOW, then just look around, the signs are all around, earth is a battleground. Spiritual leaders are rising, but it is not up to one, it is up to oneness. There is an evil rising, it is this dark force that is all around us, keeping us controlled and confined in this box. There are so many of us stumbling out of the box and when we see the place we were living in the natural response is to remove ourselves, to pull away, to become recluse. We want the positive light so we hide from the darkness. Imagine any war, if everyone that fought on either side just removed their selves from the "battlefield" it would be an easy victory.

I am not saying you have to go out with a loaded shotgun and rid the world of evil. The first step is to acknowledge that evil is present and around you. Second is to accept it, release all your fears surrounding it. Third is to prepare yourself for the spiritual warfare that may be waged against you. Fourth is to aid others in this. So many of us get stuck on the first step that it is where we are such victims. We say "oh no this world is full of evil dictators and our livelihood depends on their control over us." We become the classic conspiracy theorist and withdraw from society. If you withdraw, they have won. I spent a couple of years stuck in step one. I damaged relationships around me because I allowed this fear to overtake me. When I accepted it almost immediately I felt this lifting, this lightness, ok there is evil, I have committed evil against myself and others, I forgive myself and others for this, but I won't go down without a fight. I believe step three was the easiest for me, perhaps because step two prepared me so much for what was to come. I have had constant assault for my beliefs and I have frequently been in rooms where I was the only one standing up and saying there is a problem, which led me to step four. Disregard that you may know more than someone else, forget that and it is easier to lead. If you say I have this secret knowledge over you, then you are no different from those in control of our world right now. You are no better than anyone else and we all are born with this knowledge, we just need to remember it.

When you reach step four you step onto this battlefield, you say ok, I am ready, come and get me. I have found that I get more and more assaults that manifest financially, in interactions with people and with myself. It is a struggle no doubt, but there is a peace within myself, a calming sensation that comes when I know that I continue to fight, to allow the peaceful warrior to take over.

There are interactions with people that perhaps you never even noticed, try this, the next time you find yourself being confronted, center yourself, take a deep breath and imagine that you are holding up a mirror for the others to see themselves. It was a practice that just came to me in the midst of a strong power struggle with someone else, I saw the way I was allowing their mood to affect mine, I didn't like it so I lashed out at them, then internally came a voice, "What are you doing? You are allowing this person to take the reigns over your life!" I took a deep breath as the person continued to talk and I envisioned this mirror, almost immediately this person changed their tone, so immediate that even recalling now it gives me chills. We have this amazing power within to allow others to see themselves without saying negative things or damaging ourselves. It is something I try to practice even without confrontation, say, when a friend seeks my advice, I know that they just want to feel validated, which I don't always agree with their thoughts, so I'm not going to say, yes you're right, if I just don't agree. Instead I offer them my perspective, but while envisioning this mirror, all they want is to see them. We are so lost from who we are that we never see that and when we see it in others we freak out. Instead of looking into the mirror and saying this is what I would like to change about me, we look at others and say, this is what you need to change

Part VII

Oneness

As we separate each part of your life you must balance it with a counter intuitive reaction. You collapse them all back into one and see them as a whole. Just in practices with your chakras, while most are able to see them separately and easily grasp this concept, there comes a time when you can no longer grow from working on each separately and you must collapse them all back into one entity. One energy source that fuels your body, instead of pulling from multiple sources, then it gets confusing and you're doing more work balancing all seven versus just the one being, just as you will find it more confusing trying balancing all four parts of yourself. It is through the action of destruction of all your boundaries that you find in yourself that your higher self is also one with your lower self. Your lower self is merely your higher self, your true self clouded by low vibrations. It is through the discovery of your lower self your higher self comes to realize its true potential, through trial and err. This is why evil, why breaking, are such beautiful endeavors. The painfulness comes from your shell of darkness cracking away until the beauty of your light is left, exposed, available for the world to see, where your light is able to succeed the dark. Knowing that your lower self is a true piece of you is part of the battle, part of the awakening process. Bringing all parts of your life to one being is enlightenment. While I believe that reunification is not just limited to us but to others to be united in the oneness of life it is the path of our journey.

The term "keep your friends close, but your enemies closer," is a great ideal to see how you should face yourself when vibrating at lower frequencies. Love your lower self, for it is a part of you! If you don't learn to love your lower self and see the beauty in learning from your lower vibrations you will learn to hate it and hate is a derivative of fear, fear is a cage. Un-cage yourself! Love yourself, even when you are not maximizing your potential energy and light! If you hate when you think certain things or do certain things you become entrapped in a cage of fear. Fearful to act or think in certain ways, you become fearful of not acting according to standards, yours or the worlds. Then, it becomes all too easy to regress into all the fears of life. Learn to see the beauty in everything, including your lower self.

When you learn to love and become one with your own self you will be opened to a path to easily love others and become one with them. The whole point of oneness is to attain a flowing connection to everyone as well as yourself. Picture beams of energy flowing from you into others and from others into you. When your own energy is blocked the liquid energy in these beams becomes stagnant and just sit in you creating a cesspool, all the beams connecting you to others do the same thing. It is like a damn, the river may be strong and flowing, but once it reaches that block it sits and becomes still. You want every connection within and to the outer world to be flowing; when the energy is stagnant it opens the door to disease of the spirit which easily manifests into disease of the body.

When you see yourself you do not say, oh I am billions of cells that compose my intestines and organs; you simply say I am human. We break ourselves down into categories, but we must not miss the step of combining them back into one. You can recognize that your mind, soul, emotions and body are going to want different things for different reasons, but at the end of this journey you reunite with all those parts and you don't say I am a human that makes up the mind, soul, heart and body, you simply say, "I am one." One is an indefinite infinite statement; one can mean many, or just one. It gets complex when thinking in these terms but it also simplifies them greatly.

There's a Jewish parable a friend once told me, a man went to make fun of the Torah and said to one Rabbi, "Teach me the Torah while standing on one foot." The Rabbi got very angry and said, "There is no way I could do that." The man went on to another Rabbi to continue to mock the Torah, "Teach me the Torah on one foot." The Rabbi said, "What is hateful to you do not do to others." This is the moral to the story of our lives. The man came to the second Rabbi to poke fun at him and his beliefs and the Rabbi held true to his beliefs, taught the man and probably gave him the most astounding advice ever. It is possible to learn nothing while on one foot and yet learn everything. It is through the looking glass that you use to view the world with that will give you your whole perspective on life. Until you are ready to love yourself and others with just the basic human respect each person deserves you have learned nothing and be careful because your leg may not hold your weight for the rest of your life!

My most difficult scenarios post waking up have come from those judging myself or others. I have a friend who is spiritually awakened but his ego is still fully intact, I see him constantly judging others for their beliefs and choices. It gets me frustrated and at times I don't even want to be around him, but examining the instances and pondering it a great deal I understand that I have held the same judgments against him for his ego that he has had against me for other things in my life. I realize that the things I want to change for the better are deeply clutched in the hands of my own ego. When I feel these strong reactions instead of approaching them from a place of love, which I am striving to do, I have a tendency to tear him, or others down. The energy that fills me in these situations is like a metaphysical slap. Say you have a child and every time they say a bad word you smack them, they grow up and every time their child or someone else says a bad word they smack them. Now say you do the opposite, you use verbal communication to evaluate the choice they made, "Johnny, when you say that word what feeling are you trying to express? Why did you pick that negative word to express that you were frustrated with me?" You dialogue in a rational way and you end it with giving them the future consequence of their action, "Johnny, I love you a lot, but when you say those words I feel like you are trying to attack me. I will not allow you or anyone on earth try to attack me, if I continue to see you trying to hurt me, while I will always love you, I cannot be around someone that wants to hurt me." You explain to them what words can do to a person, but you have to tell them the consequences, not just the physical ones, "I'm going to ground you if you say that again," you tell them the impact it can have on others. When we grow up in an environment that allows you to express freely what you think and feel you do not need to use profane words to express ourselves. We learn to open our throat chakra and always tell others how we feel and think about a certain situation. If you do it in a threatening manner, even when saying positive things, they will learn this behavior of threatening others and pushing others around to get what they want to say put to the top of the priority list. Balance is key, in enforcing the positive frequencies and relinquishing ourselves and others from the negative ones. That energy that you waste on hate makes you weaker, not only because you are utilizing your energy in a negative way, but also because we are all one, when you go to attack someone else because of your differences you are attacking yourself.

There are many ways to connect in oneness with another. One of the best ways is through the Kama Sutra. When we are aligning ourselves with another and making ourselves vulnerable we shed the outer shells of deception and tap into the ability of higher growth. You are most vulnerable during sex. Like in most cases when you are the most vulnerable most risking of yourself, the ego becomes its strongest. When we engage in intercourse you are so physically exposed that it emanates deep within yourself. Things that cover us physically are things that represent deeper covers, even something like clothes, in the Garden of Eden, Adam and Eve ran and covered them in shame. We have adapted this subconsciously into every fiber of ourselves, we subconsciously cover ourselves when we put on clothes, make-up, jewelry, anything to that extent we hide ourselves physically as a way to cover up what's underneath. So when we shed those exterior covers, especially in front of someone else, our ego's want to scream, they don't like giving that control over ourselves to others, when the ego is simply the ones who give us a lack of control of ourselves. When you find someone with whom you wish to seek a deeper, more divine connection and partnership with nothing is more sacred than combining yourselves on a spiritually, mental, emotional and physical level such as the Kama Sutra Sex teaches. In Kama Sutra you are engaging both you and your partner in that deep connection. The goal of which is not climax, but the succession of ego and the journey you take with the other person. Kama Sutra is not just sensual but has the potential to be a divinely inspired adventure. The awareness you obtain during Kama Sutra Sex is so incredibly rich that it's like an upload from the source of all. This upload transpires because you are not only colliding yourself into one, you are colliding your WHOLE being with another WHOLE being. You can obtain the fulfillment of the Kama Sutra with anyone on your path.

I have wanted to try partner yoga with some friends, not for the pursuit of a sensual connection but for one that will connect our friendship and combine our separate journeys into one, if even for a glance at our oneness. When you take that step with another person, whether they are a friend, a mate, or even a stranger, you are actively preparing yourself for that collision of you with the rest of the world into the realm of oneness.

People participate in these kinds of exchanges all the time. Exchanges can be material or something more spiritual, but you must come to understand the laws guiding exchanges to be able to understand the risks involved in participation of these.

When we give gifts for birthdays, weddings, baby showers and just because, we are symbolically giving something physical in place of something deeper. Remember, we as a society have become so conditioned to perceiving the physical as the true essence when it is simply a piece. So as we grow up with this concept that physicality is real and everything else is just fantasy we come to understand how to act of ourselves in the physical sense. Each time you have given a gift you give it as a representation of your love, you subconsciously say, "Happy birthday, here is this gift that shows how delighted I am that you are here with me another year!" But what of those times when you give something of yourself that is reluctant? Your subconscious is saying, "happy birthday, I am only giving you this because you gave me a birthday present." You grow in resentment for that person and deeper, for the physical reality that places these standards on you. You shouldn't give things you feel obligated to give; you should only give of yourself, even in the physical, if it is truly within your desire to give. It is why the concept of Valentine's Day and even Christmas make me laugh; Valentine's Day is "a day of love." Yet, what happens on Valentine's Day? We expect a gift from our lovers, we expect ourselves to give a gift to our lovers, when everyone receives a gift then we are happy. If your lover forgot to buy you a gift you think, "How could he?" You beat yourself up because you think you weren't important enough to be reminder enough to receive a gift and you reflect that feeling onto your lover because they forgot. The standard for these kinds of days is so out of control it is no longer about the true gift of giving and seeing another's happiness, it has now become about getting what you want through a means not your own.

      The second way we exchange is metaphysical. I have a friend who did a meditation with his girlfriend where they decided to exchange a piece of their hearts with one another. The outcome was them ending the relationship, but they will forever be missing a piece of their hearts as well as having another person's piece attempting to fill that hole they created. I believe these types of exchanges to be very dangerous, because one, you don't know how much longer you will journey with this person, two, you don't know exactly what they are giving you with the exchange and three, you place this expectation (much like Valentine's Day) where their gift will be as great or better than yours. What if my friend had given that piece of his heart and his girlfriend didn't exchange hers? He would then have a sliver of his heart missing, not even replaced with someone else's but just missing all together. I also don't believe in placing that amount of security in anyone else, whenever you place those expectations on someone else you wind up with a sense of failure, you feel the failure even though they failed in your eyes, because you allowed yourself to be fooled by another, when in all actuality you know the risks you take.

I can see the beauty in exchanging both materially and metaphysically with another; it can be an experience through the soul of another that you cannot gain with your own perception. However, the risks being so great in these endeavors you have to be sure that they are willing to exchange with the amount you plan to exchange and you have to build a safety net for yourself so that you will not feel failed in the end. We exchange all the time, every time you change someone's life it is like you are saving them and their debt to you is subconsciously written inside of you. A piece of them goes with you just as a piece of you gets transferred to them, even on the most subconscious levels. As we exchange throughout our lives we not only exchange with that person, but we

also exchange with every person that is a part of
them.

Part VIII

Two Wild Cards

Many great stories were read to us as we were children. They all began with "once upon a time" and ended with "And they lived happily ever after." As we age and weather our physical bodies we are taught that that is not how they end. We are taught a number of things through conscious and sub-conscious repetitive messages. At a young age we are called to give up the fairy tale and believe that "that's just fantasy." But why?

I firmly believe in the happily ever after, I believe that one day our entire universe will live happily ever after. In order to achieve this, a balance must be made, this balance transcends millions of levels comparing everything from our cells to our cosmos. From relationships with others to relationships with ourselves.

It is very hard to sustain a balance in life and this is why so often we give up ever living happily. The main interferences with this balance are your ego and your free will. If everyone had no ego or free will your entire life as well as the cosmos would all be happily ever after, but they would also be happily day to day and never any growth would come.

Your Most Formidable Foe

The person who knows you best is the person who will be your greatest potential enemy. You should know this person is yourself. You know your secrets and your mistakes, your desires, your inner peace. You know regardless of whether or not you consciously are aware that you know who you are, your subconscious is quite aware. It is this, your subconscious and consciousness that work in conjunction with each other to parent over your ego. There are two types of ego, Ego and ego. Ego is that voice of compassion and confidence, your higher self, which reasons with that person that's brash and harsh. Ego comforts and boosts your confidence, it doesn't bruise easily, but we often silence it. The other, ego is quite quick to lash out and attack others and ourselves, for it is so fearful that someone else may hold an upper hand over them that it wants to put up those walls of defense against the world. It says "I will not be hurt by anyone so I will show the world how tough I am, I will attack all other people to make sure that I am salvaged!" Society has bred us to be very concerned and protected against all others, to close ourselves off from people that can hurt us and that will gain that upper hand. It is the Ego that stems from a place of love and the ego that stems from a place of fear.

I recently dealt with a person that had strong romantic emotions towards me and while he was busy planning our life together I had no idea that he was placing all these expectations of who I was and who he wanted me to be. I was very upfront with my desires for myself. After Mr. Happy I have no urge to rush into a relationship that I don't feel a divine connection with. I see that with Mr. Happy we had a divine spark and I believe he had the same, which is why our relationship flourished so quickly, but in time both of us denied ourselves our divinity for the other person and what we thought the other wanted. So coming from a place of preservation of my divinity I have made the decision to be forward with my desires for my life and not place expectations on others. While this person was really expecting me to come to an important event in his life, I had never guessed that it was so important, he didn't express his expectation of me and furthermore he made this expectation of me. Then, when I told him I couldn't attend he got very upset, he told me not to talk to him anymore. I was perplexed and felt "dumped" even though no romantic relationship was in place I never understood why he acted out in this way. I accepted his request and told him to have a great life, he became more enraged and how I could just so easily blow him off. He finally explained how he was really counting on me to be there. I have been in this position before, where you place these expectations on others, only to be crushed in the end. I have gotten, for the most part, to a point where I learn to just accept that people are completely oblivious to any of my expectations unless I voice them, even if I do tell them what's on my mind I can't hold them to have the same desires as myself. It will only set me up for failure in the end. It goes back to hoping for something better, if I just hope one day someone will come with me to a spiritual event, I would never go to a single one, I would just hope that one day someone will come. When no one comes a downward spiral ensues because I am always counting on others to gain my own happiness.

When I first stumbled upon the idea of oneness I felt this urge to hold onto the possession of everything, "but I want my own lover, I want my own mother, I want my own family, that's all mine." I was reluctant to understand the beauty of oneness, I have never felt very possessive but the concept gave me the insight of one of the biggest parts of my ego, which was my possessiveness over people. I saw it as my right to have a special relationship with my mom only, with my past loves only; even now I struggle to relinquish control. During a recent meditation I discovered some things about myself and some tools to help guide me to let go of possession over others.

First, I had to understand why I was being so possessive. I don't think I was coming from a place of negative intent. My intent was that these people are close to me and I didn't want to let that go. I wanted to forever remember the closeness and secret world I shared with each person. It was out of such deep love that I strived to hold onto each relationship, which turned into negativity, in trying to hold on I put barriers around myself, so that when I tried to hold on so tightly and strangled the person (metaphorically) I was in turn hurt that this affection wasn't reciprocated and created a wall where that relationship once was, so I would never be hurt again in the same manner. Eventually my walls towered over me and I was in such darkness that I feared every relationship and potential relationship. I feared someone taking my spot, I feared being replaced and I could only see how my replacements were nothing compared to me. In my meditation I saw how I could never be replaced, I am unique and beautiful and while others may have a closer bond to someone, they can never take my place, I am the only me that has ever existed. What a burden that was lifted! I don't need to smother others and bide for their affection, because I know that I already have it. That night I made the decision that I would never again let my fear or someone else's fear stop me from loving everyone. Everyone! Unconditional, true, divine, love. I wouldn't place expectations on others that I would be the only person in their life, I wouldn't try to outcast those that shared a secret world with the people that I had my own secret world with. I would love everyone just for being the only them I would ever meet, so unique and beautiful with everything at their fingertips to teach me.

Next, was stopping myself when I felt my ego taking over. I pondered on my outer body journey how I could recognize each person individually and see the light in them. I have already gotten in the habit of singing "All You Need Is Love" whenever I think a thought that really doesn't stem from my true self, but how would I constantly see myself and the light in others? Then a miraculous voice whispered, Namaste. Ha! I thought that's it; greet every person with Namaste every time I see them. Unlike a simple, hi, hello, it sums up the intent to honor the light within them, the beauty within them. Namaste world. You don't like me, Namaste; I see YOU and love YOU. It is a practice, I hope, that will help further my patience and love with every creature I meet. If Namaste doesn't fit for you, find a greeting you can say to others that will remind you each one of us has light and love within and that we must recognize what is within regardless of the darkness clouding the picture. The true succession of the ego is to allow everyone the same opportunities you would give each partner you have on this journey. Allow everyone to feel your love as it vibrates through you and into the world. If your ego puts a wedge between you and just one other person it becomes far too easy to allow yourself to do this to everyone else, to put so many wedges between your love and the world that no one will find out how beautiful you are.

Your Free Will

The idea of free will is that you have the free will to do whatever you wish with your life. A belief I have found to be self-evident through my life is that karma will come back to rectify the wrong you've done to others. I believe karma is expressed in two ways, one being an immediate response to you with similar consequences on you as the event you had done to someone else, typically believed to be three fold (i.e.: if you steal a hundred dollars from someone you will get 300 stolen from you), the other is that karma will represent itself to give you a chance to salvage yourself and prove you learned your lesson (i.e.: if you steal a hundred dollars from someone you will get a chance to rectify this situation by being presented with a situation where 300 dollars is sitting out on someone's counter).

You have to become aware when you are being presented with karma. Whether it's in rectification for the wrong you have done or the good. Becoming aware of the so called coincidences in your life gives you the gift to carry it into the next instance when you are being ethically tested. This is the true nature of karma.

Karma and freewill go hand in hand, when it comes to free will you have the right to do what you wish, you can get up right now and kill someone. More realistically you can get up right now and manipulate someone into doing what you want. I have had people, especially those with strong mental intuitive gifts that have used my thoughts to manipulate me to get what they wanted, simply by playing on my thoughts. In kind, I have used my empathic gifts to manipulate others. There have been times that I will send waves of emotions to others to get them to feel how I am feeling, to understand me, but in times to get something as selfish as my friend to pick the place I want to go eat. When I first became aware of this power I possessed it did go to my head. I thought "wow, look what I can do." I can't say what exactly helped me to understand that I didn't have the right to do this, beyond, well coming to understand that I don't have a fundamental right to impose on someone else's free will. No different than others have that right to do that to me. The present events are my karma coming back to me to see if I learned of the past.

There is a balance in the world and we are all responsible for keeping up our end of equilibrium. As soon as this balance is off kilter and it so often is, the universe will seek to rectify this. If you go about targeting those who are consciously weaker than you simply because you know you can gain what you want the universe will take note immediately and you will feel loss of energy, loss of self-control, in balance within, or a more physical affect such as losing something material. This is an extremely important part of consciousness, to understand that you have no right to control others. This is where a lot of people use black magic, because once you understand that there are limitless possibilities to your power and your life then you tend to react very embracing, welcoming this new gift to you. If you go down a negative path to try and make yourself feel better you will find that short term you may feel better but your energy reserves will deplete eventually and you will have to start feeding off other people's energy. You become a parasite in the world and you will one day be your own destruction.

The succession of Karma lies in everyone's hands. We have been given the tools to succeed completely from karma. Karma can be succeeded simply by forgiveness. We need to forgive ourselves the wrong things that we have done, for forgiving ourselves in this lifetime culminates with past and future lifetimes. If you acknowledge the wrong you have done, from murdering someone to stealing a piece of candy and then forgive yourself you have already prepared yourself in the next life as well as forgiven what you have done in the past lives. Forgiveness is the shortest route to living consciously, but it is one of the hardest. We must forgive ourselves, but move past that into the forgiveness of others. We are all reflections of each other and what you see in others are either past life karmic reflections or are in your present life reflections. If you take note to someone and say, "Ok you are so lazy!" Even if in this lifetime you know personally you are not lazy, the fact that you picked this out in someone else says that you had struggled with being lazy in a past life. When you forgive the other person your karma is sealed from past life incidences where you come to the knowledge that it is ok, we are all on this journey together, and we just all take separate paths.

Part IX

The Shift

There are two shifts that are taking place right now, your personal shift and the global shift. Tonight as I sat in a room meditating listening to singing bowls and receiving a Deeksha blessing around ten or so others, the two shifts collided into one shift for me. I felt the consciousness of the entire world. As we meditated it was the first time recently that I really concentrated on the higher purpose. I have been focused primarily on myself, the healing of all parts of me, so that I may better prepare myself for what is in store both personally and on a global level. I found a new way to connect to the source tonight; I actively concentrated on resonating against the singing bowls and sending that sound of peace into the world. While I sat and thought about my light going out into the world and how I was a conduit of sound and light that was amplified to all corners of the earth I thought, how much I really enjoyed the Deeksha Blessings and I would just like to experience that all my own and not try and concentrate on being that conduit and sending that blessing into the world. As I thought about it, I realized that the blessing for my personal shift could be used 100 times more than I had already experienced it if I did amplify it into the world. I opened every line of light that connected me to every soul and when it came to my turn to receive the blessing an amazing thing happened, I felt the blessing going through all my invisible links into other people and as I felt that I added my own energy to the links. I continued to meditate on. The realization was principle to me, if we were all to let every link that connects us be free flowing energy of love to other people, then the return would be that we would get back that energy amplified by everyone that is connected to us in a continuous pattern. It made complete sense, now, because we all know that the way earth is climbing up the hill to 2012 that the only way I see, is up. All our links in this earth are sending more and more love into the world. Throughout history this energy is circulated through and amplified, even if one person were to amplify the energy by a little bit it would still circulate through and resonate back with a higher frequency. The energy that you send out adds, think of a snowball rolling down a hill, it collects snow from different sources even just little flakes, but it adds and adds, the energy we send out adds and adds. This is why when people work in masses to do good, or evil, they collectively gain support, because when the energy is sent out it is magnified and returned. Think of Hitler, he had so much negative energy coming back to him that he was able to propel it off again and again to more and more people who were not in a position of light so they contributed to the snowball of the Holocaust. When we approach the global shift it is only natural that we have reached this point in history, because all that energy has to be building up to something! It's the shift that I have experienced and have seen so many experience little by little I see the sparks in each person and it makes me realize how connected we all are. Each time someone individually shifts it contributes to the global shift, the global ascension. There are some, yes, sad to say, that will not experience the shift in this life time. I do believe, that we all will come to this shift though, we all will one day will, even if it's a long time from now, shift into the true state we journey to live in. This is why I have overcome mourning for those who are still lost, I see them and I know that they are not walking my path, nor are they walking a particular easy path, but they continue to walk and persevere. They are on some kind of path, to be on a path you have to have something motivating you and no path is wrong as long as it leads you to your destination. Think of a time you got lost, you were driving around frantic and scared of the unknown possibilities, much like being lost on a path in life; we wander scared and frantic, trying to find our way out. Sometimes we add to these fearful feelings and we manifest the worst, but when you trust that you will find the easier path or the ultimate destination it manifests to allow you to find where you are going.

Just through positive intent and positive thoughts we begin to see paths come across ours that are easier and easier to walk. It is our intent that will not only lighten our load but the loads of others, because all you have to do is take off the weight from yourself and someone still burdened by the weight of the world will feel their load become lighter.

The destination is not a final stop, it continues on infinitely, just as in life you reach a destination but you do not stop there, you continue on; from there you leave again and go somewhere else. Our spirits are wanderers whether or not you enjoy wandering in the physical realm our spirits enjoy new endeavors and adventures.

We, in this world, must become like the spirit, transparent to all, for you will be faced with adversaries that will say "aha! I found out your flaw, I know your secret," if we are not transparent then we will become fearful that our flaws will be seen by the world. Allow yourself to be so transparent that no secrets hold you captive and that everyone may see you for who you are, so that no one will ever have an upper hand. Transparency also prevents things to become stuck to you, because you can see them so easily that when someone tries to put a label or something on you, you can see it. Evaporate into the vast sea of nothingness, of consciousness, you will not lose yourself, but only shift into a higher state of awareness, you will become like fog that cannot get stuck on anything, move freely through the world and where you want to go.

Let go! Let go of the façade you wear, let go of your fears and anxieties, let go and nothing will be able to keep you or anchor you down. You will be freed from pain and open to only light if you just let go. I struggle with this daily and I feel it human nature to do so. We all desperately want to be freed but have been conditioned to believe all the woes of the world were caused by us; truly, we just crave the love that our souls derive from. We do not need to suffer in order to receive this. Close your eyes and meditate on your body, see what needs light and what is already receiving light. This may take a long time and I still have not perfected what ritual for me works best in this respect, but have come closer to understanding through feeling where the energy stops flowing. My solar plexus is so open and I have become so much more aware of this that when even the slightest bit of it closes it feels like a huge knot in my stomach. On my journey I have met many who this examination comes very easy, I have a friend who easily feels others blocks, but he cannot find a way to connect it to his mind. I have met others with this same issue, but when I see them I don't see a weakness, I see a great empathic strength that I wish I could manifest right now. I know in time if I continue this path I will be reaching this point, but it doesn't feel soon enough. Time is certainly speeding up, it seems as though it is flying by, I want my growth to speed with the time, but can't seem to adjust quickly enough. I have had breakthroughs in my life that others have been so quick to say I am lucky to have, but my self-doubt throughout life has led me to struggle so greatly with the gifts I have been given. I have become more confident in my intuition, but I still have doubts, I find the only time I receive extra gifts is when I let go. When I detach myself from the desire or need to obtain a certain goal it comes so easily! The harder I try to reach certain milestones the further away it goes. During meditations I often see things then try and focus on them, when I do this it evaporates like a hologram. When I focus on my third eye too intensely I see an "angry eye" appear, when I am not consciously focusing I receive many images. There have been times when I am able to harness the energy and put it towards good use. The trick is to (1) have positive intent, the more positive the quicker the growth and the more you will receive from the experience, (2) release pressure, understand that if you do not receive the desired outcome, you will one day, do not be too attached to the outcome that it disrupts other goals you have attained in life and (3) do it because you want to, too often I try and do things because someone else can and it becomes about the ego and less derived from love. If you have the intention in your heart, whether it for you or another and you want to, it will come naturally, just give it room to breathe and manifest!

As your shift begins to take place, understand that where you are today will be drastically more aware from yesterday, the day before, the week before, the year. We are all shifting and as long as your shift is coming from a place from positive intent and with love you will easily ascend. When you strike that AHA moment you may say, this is it, this is transcendental. Truth is, the highest you are now is still not your full potential, we are infinite beings and it is impossible to place any finite spectrums on us.

Picture it as a spiral, we start on the outside working inward, that AHA moment is a fixed point that cuts through the entire spiral and as it circles in you reach it quicker and quicker each time. Bringing yourself closer and closer to the final point, but what may seem like the final point in the spiral only continues deeper and deeper into you.

Closing

Throughout this past year of writing I have had the opportunity to reflect so much and grow on my initial base when I started this journey. The journey is nowhere near complete, but this phase of my life, this book, is. It is a sacred guide, if at the least to me. It has grown like a person grows, with me. It has been my counselor and my teacher. I often would sit down to write and would just let everything flow freely. I sometimes go through and read things and go "Wow, how did that profound statement came from me?" I felt as though a lot of my book wasn't written by me, that there was a Divine presence utilizing my hands to type. I was speaking with a friend of the mounting pressure I felt to edit and change things in this book, due to how drastic my life and belief system has changed in this short time. I didn't want for readers to feel confused at where I was coming or going. I wanted it to be pliable in the smallest sense of leading others to doors to open for themselves. She gave me a piece of advice that I have taken to heart, to allow my book to reflect that growth and not try and edit my life. I have allowed this book to really have its own creative growth and anticipate that it perhaps can grow with the readers that these crazy confusing concoctions of writings will have aged in beliefs with you. I have travelled through life in crazy instances that I felt so alone in for so long. It was only through seeing others that loneliness became a perception and only that. That I only perceived I was alone to play up the victim role.

I feel that a natural question that may arise is my secular beliefs. I believe that as a reader you may feel compelled to agree with me just because of my beliefs or may feel compelled to ignore what I am saying because of them. I feel as though I am an evolving consciousness. My beliefs are from experiences, what works in my life, versus what doesn't. What resonates with my soul versus what doesn't.

As I have stated I was raised Catholic, I felt a discontent all my life with this. I began seeking new religions that fit, I feel like I tried everything. I studied and became a sponge seeking what was "right." I went from Catholic, to Buddhism, to non-denominational Christian, to Catholic, to Hinduism, to Esoteric Christianity, to where I am at now. Every church I went to, every book by a secular organization and every person I met regarded their beliefs as supreme. They all told me why the others were wrong and why I would find value in their beliefs. I made this extensive chart comparing all these religions, I think there was about 70 Abrahamic religions (Islamic, Christian and Judaism) on the chart as well as some other bigger polytheistic religions. I found that their beliefs so intertwined and when talking to an Atheist he said that, "It's all about morality, they're stories of morality," while I believe there is deeper meaning in scriptures and traditions than this, I definitely agree with what he said to some extent. Our peace in life is in believing that we are walking "the correct path." We get angry when these beliefs are challenged because we believe so deeply in them. From what I have studied I see that there are so many contradictions, editing and translational errors that happen in most religions. I am not against religious principles or those who seek that lifestyle; I am against these beliefs confining or controlling you, or any beliefs for that matter.

For instance, if I say my belief is in karmic philosophy, solely that whatever I do negative will be punished three fold, whatever positive will come back as well and that some higher power is punishing me and rewarding me for my actions as my life ages. I will then see every negative action that ever happens to me as a punishment for doing something negative to another, every positive as a reward for doing something positive. I become untrue to my heart, because I want the reward and not because I feel like doing something nice for another. In kind, I become fearful of negative things happening to me, so I do everything in my power to suppress the "negative," from thoughts to action. This denial of human experience is something that I believe comes from our interaction with our belief system. If we deny what is truth in our heart then we have massive explosions in our emotions, we become suppressed and confined by fear. This is not to say that it does not provide beneficial by others, that this stability is not comforting.

I believe, that the earth is our mother and the cosmic consciousness our father. From the two we were created. We are brothers and sisters and all connected. I believe that the earth is a consciousness, that she feels pain and responds to this. I believe that our God Head, or father, our cosmic consciousness, interacts with our life in the space that he oversees what we do, he may teach us lessons, positive and negative, but he doesn't dictate to us what we are to do. I believe that we can feel everyone and tap into any given person on this planet or in the afterlife at any given time, if it is so that we desire. I believe that the teachings in most Holy Scriptures are sacred, that they do have much to teach us. I also believe man has manipulated these texts to exert power over others and that these teachings are riddled with hidden meanings. These teachings have to be read in a certain light to protect them, when a lot of these texts were created they were at times when you could be killed very quickly for your beliefs, so the meat of the teachings are hidden in symbolism.

I believe that Jesus, is son of God, I believe we are all children of God and as it states in The Bible, we are all capable of walking on water and moving mountains, if we have that faith we can do so. I have had six separate occasions in the past two years where Jesus and I have interfaced. Once, on Mother's Day 2010, which the book covers on, in a dream. Another during a Singing Bowl Meditation, sometime in early 2011, I saw him for a fleeting moment, the guy sitting next to me remarked after the meditation that he felt him. During my first Heart Chakra Trance Dance, I believe in May or June 2011, I saw Jesus, Mother Theresa, Ghandi, Martin Luther King, Buddha and a slew of other Prophets of love; I felt their radiating love for humanity and I felt the course of their actions. Their intentions behind why they did what they did for us. I had another dream after my second Heart Chakra Trance Dance, where I was speaking to the Divine Source; He was explaining to me the course of how his Prophets were chosen. He told me that he selected those that most reflected Him in His true essence. That these were people that had a certain awareness to them that could lead the world into a place of self-creation rather than self-destruction. I then saw and felt each individual Prophet, hundreds upon thousands, old and new, I understood them all, they passed this little wafer, what I can best describe as a host you would take during communion, they passed it down the line of the thousands of them until it got to me, I grinned a childish grin and ate it. The second to last time I saw Jesus and interacted with him was during the third Heart Chakra Trance Dance I attended in July 2011. I was projected, as if I was living it out, to His crucifixion. Around me there were men that watched with sorrow and women that were violently weeping. I had tears streaming down my face as well, I was a part of this small group of women watching, holding each other as we were hysterically collapsing on one another. We watched his flesh pierced by the nails. Jesus looked resolved; he looked more concerned over us, than himself. His face began to lose color as they rose up the cross, his head hung back his eyes stared directly in mine, as everyone around me was in chaos he met me, it was as if he was saying, this is the reason. His eyes told me that he was not afraid of the next life, that he was happy to be there, but that his heart felt pain for leaving us. They raised him up fully and we sat under the shadow which faded as the rain rolled in, washing down his blood and the dirt from his body upon the earth. My final interaction through visions with Jesus came from my Crown Chakra Trance Dance in October 2011 where I was dancing in a barren dirt covered wasteland. The ground was dry and the sun was hot, there was but one sign of life a bonsai tree in the distance. As I twirled around the desert something in the distance began walking towards me. Though this place was not the ideological vision of a happy place for me, there wasn't a care in the world. I continued to dance and the mirage became closer and clearer, it was a group of people walking hand and hand, all smiling. As they grew nearer it was my prophets, with Jesus in the middle. It was as though they had been marching and saying, "this is it, we are all here now, no more fears, no more pain, this is the new world. It is bare to provide for a new beginning that we write, see that tree, it is sign that life can thrive here and we will all be a part of this!" There were drums and cheering coming from somewhere, it was a beautiful sight! Exuberant celebration!

I believe that we are capable of miraculous things, just that we need the right motivation to achieve this. I believe in manifestation, both of negative and positive. I believe in our ability to know everything, just we have forgotten. I believe that you can have Divine interaction in everything in your life. I believe in Divine presence in everything. I believe that hurting others hurts you. I believe that peace comes from within. I believe that there are dark forces, but they are capable of salvation and being brought to the light. I believe that we all have our separate paths but the end goal is the same. I believe there will come a time that we are all liberated from fear and I believe this time is growing near.

My intent for this book is that it provides a truthful look at one journey. That you may be able to walk away with some sort of insight on how to change things in your life or how to better apply things, whether or not it is in alignment with anything that I have said. I never want anything I say to become fact in anyone's life or to be used against another; I merely want to inspire your own cultivation. Whatever that looks like, let you be guided and follow your own instincts, see beauty in the negative and positive, honor yourself. If you agree with the book good for you, if you disagree, good for you. Whether I challenged a belief in you to cause you to better represent that idea or verified a belief you have held I hope this was a catalyst on any level for your life!

I am open to my beliefs changing and evolving because as I have seen them evolve in the past I know that the worst time for me could be when they seize to evolve, when they remain stagnant and unchangeable. I take every piece of wisdom that has come into my life, from the unspeakable to the very vocal and incorporate it to my belief system. I uphold that these beliefs are to be challenged and grow in my understanding. I try to be slippery in life, uncontainable and a part of everything. My understanding is that questioning your reality leads to a better awareness, so I'm always going to be questioning everything. Curiosity is healthy and change is inevitable. If I hold on to a collapsing world or belief then I collapse with it, if I allow myself to move freely in and out of the worlds and beliefs then I become one, with all. Perfectly imperfect.

You are standing on the shore...

I want to thank so many people for helping me cultivate this beautiful garden I call a book. I couldn't have gotten anywhere without the love and support of those who have come to know me on my journey….

♥

Kayla, my dear *cousin*, remember memories and love is always thicker than blood! That being said, you, my dear, are the biggest inspiration my entire life has ever known. I cannot even fathom your journey, but I see you walking it every day and love you for that!

♥

For my mommy, who brought all 9 lbs. 4 ounces of me into this world. Who has stuck by my side through thick and thin and has never turned her back on me, my best friend in this world and the next!

♥

For Chicard who has helped me come to know this reality as a farce and has given me someone to whom I can be brutally honest with and know it will not change our relationship!

♥

For the rest of my family which there are many too many to name, but all whom hold a deep sincere place in my subconscious and conscious, all who have taught me patience, devotion, love and strength, you are the ones who have walked most with me on my path.

♥

For my Boo and my Dopey both of whom hold dear places in my heart, for the love you each have given me and the extreme amount of patience while putting up with my rollercoaster life! Thank you for every step you each have taken with me!

♥

To Bobiloohoo, my dear companion, I am so blessed to have met a woman with strength and beauty as strong as yours! Thank you for being my substitute grandma as well as my caring friend!

To Charlie, my funky spiritual leader with a wise soul and a young heart you have been my mentor both in this reality and the spiritual one. Thank you for counseling me through broken hearts, spiritual battles and just the everyday pains of life!

♥

To my Yogi Laura, whose empathic intuition has helped me to embrace that fundamental side of me! Who has brought me into a passionate loving relationship with my body to the depths of my soul!

♥

To my "Guru," Lynne may that word tremble deep within your soul and then may you come to the beautiful realization of how much energy you have fed into my life, how many platforms you have held for me to grow upon, the spaces you have kept sacred, the layers you have let me unpeel and the pains you have helped me cast away all have pieces of you in them. Satnam my friend!

♥

To Tony and Stephen the dynamic duo that have guided me to wondrous heights! I found a new me through the blessings of sound and energy you both have shed to me! May those blessed with your presence always be filled with the abundance of love that has filled me in your meditations.

♥

To my past loves, my present loves and those who may be in the future; you have given, are giving and will give me the exact balance and dose of reality I need.

♥

To AM, I only get the chills when I'm with you.

♥

Printed in Great Britain
by Amazon